VOLUME 1 Ancient Israel to 1880's America

THE History of the Jewish People

A Story of Tradition and Change

by Ellen Bari

Behrman House Publishers
www.behrmanhouse.com

Project Manager: Gila Gevirtz

Designer: Stacey May

Cartographic Consultant: Dr. Itzik Eshel

The Publisher gratefully acknowledges the cooperation of the following sources of photographs and graphic images: American Jewish Historical Society: 49; Beth Hatefusoth Museum of the Jewish Diaspora: 17; Corbis: magnifying glass on each "Learning Objectives" feature; Creative Images: right-hand photograph on each "Family Connection" feature; Gustav Doré: 12; Gila Gevirtz: 9, 21, 34, 63; The Granger Collection, NY: 44; Richard Lobell: left-hand image on each "Family Connection" feature; Jim McMahon 24, 32, 36, 51, 56, 66, 70, 76; Elizabeth Reade Photography: 26.

Springfield, New Jersey

www.behrmanhouse.com

ISBN 10: 0-87441-191-2

ISBN 13: 978-0-87441-191-1

Manufactured in the United States of America

Contents

INTRODUCTION

Structure of the Textbook

The History of the Jewish People: A Story of Tradition and Change, Volume 1, was developed and written by two esteemed scholars, Professors Jonathan D. Sarna and Jonathan B. Krasner. It provides students in grades 5 through 7 with a rich, interactive presentation of history from our earliest ancestors in the Land of Israel to our dispersion in the Diaspora to the Jewish experience in America in the 1880's. Each chapter helps students consider how their lives compare with the lives of our ancestors, how each generation adapts Judaism to its time and place, and how the decisions of our forebears influence our own lives and decisions.

Jewish history comes alive through a dynamic array of famous personalities, diverse source material, clear and concise charts, engaging activities, thought-provoking questions, and exciting graphics, including sixteen maps and more than one hundred full-color historical and contemporary images.

Each chapter of the textbook includes core information that presents the time period and theme of the chapter. The themes relate to how Jews in the period under discussion adapted Judaism to meet the needs and opportunities of their time. Each chapter also includes the features listed below.

The Big Picture: Presents an overview and sets the stage for the chapter theme and content.

Investigate: Poses questions for students to explore as they read.

Key Words and Places: Highlights core words and places that are critical to understanding the chapter.

Map: Helps students place the historic period in geographic context.

Famous Figures: Spotlights a famous person from the historic period.

Then & Now: Encourages students to reflect on what they have learned and compare and contrast the chapter's historical period with our own time.

In addition, throughout each textbook chapter there are a variety of sidebars with engaging enrichments and creative opportunities for student interaction and reflection. For example, in chapter 4, "Rabbinic Judaism," the "Prayer House Plus" activity (page 45) gives students an opportunity to create a flyer describing their synagogue. They are also asked to imagine distributing the flyer in a Judean marketplace and to consider what might be familiar and unfamiliar about their synagogue to a Jew living in that time.

A glossary and detailed index are available at the back of the book.

Structure of the Teaching Guide

This teaching guide is designed to help you enhance and build upon the information and activities that are found in the textbook. It includes a variety of activities that offer students a rich and meaningful learning experience: probing questions that stimulate critical thinking and class discussion, collaborative learning environments, and creative activities for in-class and family participation. In addition, it uses a range of learning modalities, including music, art, role-playing, journaling, and debating. Where appropriate, the teaching guide provides answers to questions in the textbook.

Most important, the suggestions in the teaching guide can be easily adapted to your personal teaching style and to the strengths and interests of your students. To help you succeed, when selecting an activity, consider the many factors that come into play in your class, such as time constraints and students' abilities, interests, experience, and maturity level.

Each chapter in the teaching guide complements a chapter in the textbook and includes the elements listed below.

Core Concepts: A brief summary of the chapter's central, governing ideas.

Learning Objectives: Goals for students to achieve by the end of the chapter.

Chapter Overview: A brief statement about the chapter content.

Teaching Opportunities: Practical suggestions for introducing the chapter as well as teaching tips, activities, and discussion ideas to enrich student learning.

Using This Teaching Guide

Before you begin to teach a textbook chapter, skim or read through the material in the corresponding chapter of this teaching guide so that you can select the activities you want to pursue with your students. Many of the questions posed in the textbook and teaching guide are open-ended and personal in nature and lend themselves to a multitude of appropriate responses. Use these questions to encourage discussion and the sharing of personal ideas, opinions, and experiences.

Remember that it is the relationship your students have with you and their classmates that will largely determine the success of the learning environment. Make it clear that your classroom is a safe space where students will be heard with respect and be guided, not judged. When a student prefers not to share, it is usually best to respect his or her privacy.

Teaching History with Timelines

You can use the chapter timelines as a way of previewing each chapter with your students. Have students read the timeline information and discuss the people, places, and events with which they are familiar and those about which they want to learn more. Before each class you may ask for a volunteer or several volunteers to research information about one or more of the people, places, or events. Students may do their research on the Internet or in the synagogue library, public library, or home library, and then share their findings with the class.

Over the course of the semester or year, you may want to create a timeline with the class based on the timelines in the book. Include events from world history for each time period. If you choose, you can make your timeline modular, using 8 1/2 x 11 sheets of paper, so that it literally grows as you continue to progress through time. Alternatively, you can use a large sheet of butcher-block paper or create a timeline on the computer.

Students can limit their entries to the events listed on the textbook's timeline or they may do research and expand the information. They can embellish the timeline by adding drawings or other graphic images.

Consider assigning each timeline update to a different student or group of students. The student or group may present the class with a quick update at the beginning of the lesson.

Teaching History with Maps

The maps in *The History of the Jewish People* are designed to help students more fully imagine and understand the historic periods they study. Many provide detailed information on the migration of Jews from one area of the world to another and on critical events and changing cultural influences. This teaching guide will help you develop your students' map reading and interpretation skills, including their ability to

- Discuss information presented in the map format.
- Identify recurring elements in maps as well as what is new or similar to prior maps.
- Develop a sense of place based on maps.

Depending on your own comfort level and the interest and knowledge of your students, spend as much or as little time exploring the maps as you like.

Creating a Family Connection

At the end of each chapter in this teaching guide are opportunities to involve families in your students' learning process. You may want to send a note to parents and guardians at the beginning of the school year to introduce them to the family activities to which they will be invited. A sample letter is shown on page 7.

Shalom,

This year our class will study Jewish history using the first volume of *The History of the Jewish People: A Story of Tradition and Change.* This lively and colorful textbook was written by two leading scholars, Professors Jonathan Sarna and Jonathan Krasner. Along with learning the major events and personalities that shaped the lives of our forebears, we will also explore the diverse ways in which the Jewish people have adapted and continue to adapt to changing times and circumstances.

To reinforce what your child has learned and to help your child assimilate this new knowledge, you will be invited periodically to participate in an activity. Your participation will help affirm the importance of your child's religious school studies by linking your family values and traditions to the material we are studying. In some cases, you may want to read the textbook chapter with your child, search the Internet for additional information, or use our synagogue's library to deepen your understanding of the subject.

I hope you will find the activities engaging and enjoyable and that they stimulate meaningful family dialogue and enrich your child's appreciation of Jewish life and tradition.

Thank you for your interest.

Sincerely,

Wishing you and your students every success.

TEACHING TECHNIQUES

Building on Students' Prior Knowledge

You can introduce your class to the first volume of *The History of the Jewish People* by building on students' knowledge. Begin by distributing the book and asking what the title, subtitle, and cover images suggest the book will be about. Then invite students to read the table of contents and skim the textbook, so that they can offer additional thoughts on what it is about.

page vi **Why Study Jewish History?**

Invite several volunteers to each read a paragraph. Read the photo caption and discuss the photograph. Ask students if they have ever met a Jew from Scotland or if they are surprised that there are Jews in Scotland. Invite students to name countries in which famous Jews or Jews they know have lived. List the names of the countries on the chalkboard. *(Yitzhak Rabin/Israel, Anne Frank/Holland, grandmother/Morocco)*

Ask: Why do you think the book says that "you will discover that you are not just *studying* our people's extraordinary journey—you are also *part of the action*"? *(How we live will become Jewish history someday. The decisions we make will affect what happens to the Jewish people.)*

Invite students to write about what might be said about them in a Jewish history textbook one hundred years from now. Encourage them to think big and to write about the roles they would like to play in the story of our people!

page 1 **How Do We Do It?**

After reading and discussing the page, have students point out what in the Passover seder photograph looks the same as seders they have attended and what looks different.

For fun and to whet their appetite for the book, read aloud the story on page 161. Later in the year, when students reach that chapter, have them reread the piece and answer the questions.

Tell students that as they read *The History of the Jewish People*, they will have many opportunities to consider when and how they might learn from the experiences and decisions of our ancestors, and how they themselves want to contribute to the ongoing story of the Jewish people.

Introduction

The Birth of Our People and Monotheism

textbook pages 2–5

Overview

The early history of the Israelites and their religious beliefs are presented. Despite similarities to their neighbors, who believed in many gods, our ancestors distinguished themselves by their monotheistic beliefs.

core concepts

- Monotheism fostered the Israelites' development of a strong ethical code.
- Today we are guided by the same core ethical values as our ancestors.

Learning Objectives

Students will be able to

- Identify primary differences between the early Israelites and their ancient neighbors: the concept of monotheism and the Torah.
- Describe the Torah, as a moral and ethical code, the centerpiece of the Jewish value system.
- Apply what they have learned to explain one way in which our ancestors have influenced our own lives.

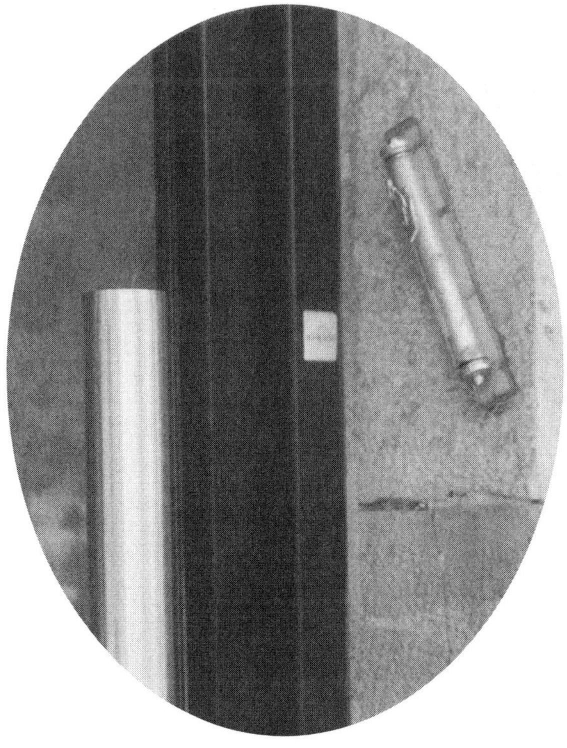

Teaching Opportunities

Getting Started

Supplies you will need: world map, tape, and one strip of construction paper for each student. Tape a world map to the wall. Using the map, have students locate where they live. Ask: Where did our earliest ancestors live? *(Ancient Israel)* Ask: How do we know? *(The Bible and archaeological remains tell us.)*

Provide each student with a strip of paper and a piece of tape. Have each one write his or her name on the strip. Ask one student at a time to use one hand to cover his or her eyes, then guide the student to the map and invite him or her to tape the strip on Israel. Students quickly will see how difficult it is to locate the right spot. The student who tapes his or her strip closest to Israel wins.

Ask: If Israel is so tiny, why is it so important? *(Israel is the homeland of the Jewish people; out of Israel and the Jewish people have come important ideas, such as the idea of one God and the teachings of the Torah, that have influenced the world.)*

Tell students that they will learn about the early importance of Israel in the history of our people and the history of the world.

page 2 **As Numerous as the Stars**

Explain that Israelites, children of Israel, and *b'nei Yisrael* are all terms that refer to the same people.

page 2 **Learning Your BCES**

Invite a student to read this feature. Explain that dates before the common era are always labeled BCE but that, generally, dates from the common era are not labeled. For example, today when an e-mail or letter is dated, it is not labeled CE.

page 3 **Map: The Israelite Tribes and Their Neighbors**

Name the neighbors of the ancient Israelites. *(Phoenicians, Hivites, Arameans, Canaanites, Ammonites, Moabites, Edomites, Amalekites)*

Compare the map on page 3 to a modern map of Israel. Have students identify cities and bodies of water that appear on both maps. *(Jaffa [may be spelled Yaffo], Ashkelon, Gaza, Hebron, Jerusalem, Beit-Shean, Mediterranean Sea, Sea of Galilee, Dead Sea, Jordan River)*

page 4 **The Gift of Monotheism**

Have volunteers read aloud one paragraph each of this section. Ask students what prayer comes to mind when they think of the Jewish people's belief in one

God. *(the Sh'ma)* Point out the photo at the bottom of page 5 and have students read the caption. Ask if anyone knows the prayer in Hebrew. *(Sh'ma Yisrael, Adonai Eloheinu, Adonai eḥad.)*

page 5 **You Are There: A Conflict of Cultures**

What pressure might you feel to worship Ba'al? *(Peer pressure, desire to participate in local holidays and celebrations)* Encourage students to talk or write about an incident in which they felt conflicted between their religious and secular interests or commitments, such as religious school classes that took place during soccer practice, and how they handled it. Keep the conversation nonjudgmental but encourage students to see how they can make choices that enable them to participate in both Jewish and secular life.

1 The Early Israelites

Adapting to a Changing World

textbook pages 6–15

Chapter Overview

A kingdom was built in ancient Israel. It split in two and eventually was destroyed. Many Israelites were forced out of their homeland, yet some returned to rebuild it, even as others remained in the Diaspora to flourish in foreign lands. Both those who lived in Israel and those who lived in the Diaspora adapted Judaism to their changing circumstances.

core concepts

- As their circumstances changed, the Israelites changed their way of life.
- Despite the many adaptations they made, both in Israel and in exile, our ancestors maintained their core religious beliefs and identities.
- Our ancestors' ability to balance the need for change with their commitment to Jewish tradition continues to inspire us.

Learning Objectives

Students will be able to

- Explain how our ancestors adapted Judaism in the Land of Israel and in the Diaspora.
- Describe at least two practices that helped our ancestors to maintain their religious identities in the Diaspora.
- Apply what they have learned to explain how these adaptations continue to influence our lives today.

Teaching Opportunities

Getting Started
Ask students to imagine that they are going on a long trip that will last several years. Tell them that they can take only two items with them to help them maintain their Jewish identities and live as Jews. Ask: What items would you take and why would you choose them? Have students work independently and have them write their answers on slips of paper. Put the papers into a hat so that the writers remain anonymous. Have one volunteer read the responses and another write them on the chalkboard. Put marks next to responses that recur. Discuss what might be the reasons why some of the items were selected by several people. (Alternatively, rather than using slips of paper, you can have students just share and discuss their responses and reasons.)

Tell the class that in this chapter they will learn about how our ancestors maintained their Jewish identities when they were forced to leave the Land of Israel.

pages 6–7, 9 **The Big Picture** and **Illustration: David and Goliath**
Individually or as a class have students read "The Big Picture." Ask students what biblical story they think is illustrated on pages 6–7. Note: The image can more fully be seen on page 9. *(David and Goliath)* Ask students how the picture might relate to the text they just read. *(David became king of Israel.)*

pages 3, 8 **Map: The Israelite Tribes and Their Neighbors** and **Deborah of Lappidoth**
For this activity, you will need one Bible for every two or three students. Chapter 5 of the Book of Judges presents a poem by the judge Deborah. It celebrates her army's victory. Have students work collaboratively in small groups or request volunteers to each read one verse aloud from a portion of that poem, Judges 5:14–18. Ask students to turn to the map on page 3 of the textbook. Using the map as a reference, ask which of the tribes are mentioned in the verses. *(Ephraim, Benjamin, Zebulun, Issachar, Reuben, Dan, Naphtali)*

pages 8–9 **A Kingdom Is Built but Cracks**
Quickly review the story of David and Goliath (found in the Book of Samuel, chapter 17), the slingshot-flinging boy who triumphs against an armored giant. Discuss the illustration at the top of page 9. Point out that the king at the top of the page is King Saul, Goliath is the large figure on the ground, and David is the

figure with the sword. (After felling Goliath with a stone, David took Goliath's sword from its sheath and beheaded him [Samuel 17:51].)

Have each student write a perspective journal entry, telling the story of David and Goliath as one of the following personalities: David preparing for battle; Goliath looking at his "unworthy" opponent; an Israelite bystander who witnessed the battle. Invite students to read their entries to the class and discuss how and why the perspectives vary.

page 10 **Map: Judah Under Changing Empires**

Using the information from the map's legend, have students calculate how long each empire ruled Judah. Which empire ruled longest? *(Persian Empire)* Which covered the most territory? *(Persian Empire)* Using the scale at the bottom of the map, calculate the distance from Jerusalem to Babylon. *(approximately seven hundred miles)* To give students a more concrete sense of the distance, you may want them to locate a city seven hundred miles from their hometown on a map of North America.

page 12 **By the Rivers of Babylon**

Materials: One copy of Psalm 137 for each member of the class, enough drawing paper and drawing materials, such as crayons and colored pencils, for the class. Before reading the psalm, explain that a lyre is an ancient stringed musical instrument and that *palate* refers to the roof of the mouth. Have volunteers each read one verse aloud. After discussing the mood and meaning of the poem, invite students to draw an illustration to accompany the psalm, portraying the sense of loss, sorrow, or loyalty to Jerusalem that it expresses. The drawings can be used to decorate a bulletin board or scanned into the computer and displayed on your synagogue's Web site along with the words of Psalm 137.

pages 10–12 **A Message of Hope**

Write this quote on the blackboard: "…and they shall beat their swords into plowshares, and their spears into pruning hooks. Nation shall not lift up sword against nation; neither shall they learn war any more" (Isaiah 2:4). Tell the class that these words of the prophet Isaiah are etched into a special wall across from the United Nations in New York City. Ask: Why do you think it was placed next to the UN? How might these words inspire world leaders?

page 13 **To Stay or Not to Stay**

Decades earlier the Jews had wept for their lost homeland. Now many in Babylonia were passing up the opportunity to return to the Land of Israel and take part in the reconstruction of their nation and the *Beit Hamikdash*. How could this be? Some answers can be found by comparing the experience of this ancient Jewish community to the modern *kibbutz galuyot*, or ingathering of the exiles, which took place after the creation of the modern State of Israel in 1948.

In the 1940's and 1950's, as soon as immigration to Israel was permitted, the new country was flooded with newcomers, or *olim*. But the vast majority were poor or had been oppressed in their countries of origin—refugees from the Holocaust or Jews from Arab lands. Jews who shared in the freedom and prosperity of more affluent countries, such as the United States, Canada, England, and Australia, were far less likely to uproot themselves and start life over again in the new Jewish state.

Invite students to talk to older members of their family or community. Ask them to find out where these people were living in 1948 and whether or not they had considered settling in Israel at the time. Ask what factors influenced their decisions. In addition, some students may have parents who lived in or visited Israel more recently. Their experiences and thoughts may also enrich the class discussion.

page 13 **To Stay or Not to Stay**

In 1985 a joint effort called "Operation Moses" was sponsored by the Jewish communities of North America and Israel to help save the Jews of Ethiopia from oppression and famine by airlifting them to Israel. In 1991, with many Ethiopian Jews still in Ethiopia, "Operation Solomon" airlifted an additional fourteen thousand Ethiopian Jews to Israel.

Below are two learning opportunities that can enrich students' understanding of what it means to leave a place with which you are familiar in order to return to the Jewish homeland.

On page 31 of *The New American Haggadah* (Behrman House, 1999) Kessaye Tevajieh, an Ethiopian Jew, describes how it felt to make the decision to leave Ethiopia. Read and discuss her story with the class.

Shlomo Gronich, a well-known Israeli musician, formed the Sheba Choir, whose members are children from Ethiopia. The choir performs music that blends the many musical traditions that are in Israel today. Some of the songs the Sheba Choir sings tell of the difficulties and conflicts in leaving Ethiopia and coming to Israel. Ask your synagogue librarian or cantor if he or she has the CD *Shlomo Gronich & the Sheba Choir*. You can share the CD and story of the Ethiopian Jews with your class.

page 13 **Returning and Rebuilding**

Invite two volunteers to the front of the class to play the following roles on a panel: a person who has decided to stay in Babylonia and one who has returned to Israel. Encourage the volunteers to think about the factors that might have influenced their decisions, for example, concerns about family including elderly relatives and young children, financial concerns, language barriers, Israel in ruins.

Give both students several minutes to explain the reasons for their choices, i.e., to remain in the Diaspora or resettle in the Land of Israel. Then invite the class to pose questions to the panelists. Afterward, open up the discussion to the entire class. Have students discuss the decisions they think they might have made had they lived under the Persians. Encourage them to explain their reasons.

page 15

Then & Now

Divide the class into groups of two or three students. Ask each group to discuss the following question: How can religious rituals like keeping kosher, performing a baby naming, or observing the Shabbat strengthen community ties? *(They often bring people together physically and spiritually; they create common experiences and interests among people in the community.)*

Family Connection

If students know the *haftarah* portions they will be studying for their bar or bat mitzvah service, invite them to research with their families information about the prophet associated with their *haftarah* portions. Instruct them to find out more about the prophet—who the prophet was and what the prophet did and taught. If students have not yet been assigned their *haftarah* portions, then have them research one of the prophets known for his ethical teachings, such as Isaiah, Jeremiah, and Ezekiel. Encourage family members to consider what they think is the greatest teaching or lesson of the prophet they research.

2 The Age of Hellenism

Diverse Strategies for Survival

textbook pages 16–27

Chapter Overview

The lure and force of Hellenism polarized the Jews of Israel. The three alternative reponses were resistance, assimilation, and accommodation. For the most part, the Diaspora Jews chose to accommodate to Hellenism while maintaining their religious identity and their ties to the Jews of Judea. While ultimately regaining their independence under the Hasmoneans, the ongoing influence of Hellenism in the region remained a challenge to the Jewish state.

core concepts

- The Jews responded to the challenge of Hellenism with diverse strategies: resistance, assimilation, and accommodation.
- We continue to use diverse strategies in facing the challenges of our own time.

Learning Objectives

Students will be able to

- Identify at least two temptations that existed for Jews to adopt Hellenistic ways.
- Describe at least two things that helped the Jews resist the temptation to assimilate.
- Apply what they have learned to explain how our lives today mirror those of our ancestors.

Teaching Opportunities

Getting Started

Ask your class to imagine that a new principal in their school now requires all students to wear the school colors—orange and blue—to school every day. Divide students into three groups: resisters, assimilators, adapters. Their positions are as follows: The first group ignores, or resists, following the ruling. The second group agrees to follow the ruling and blend in, or assimilate. And the third group is willing to compromise, or adapt.

Give each group five minutes to develop an explanation in support of the position it represents. Bring the class back together and have a volunteer from each group explain its reasoning. *(Resisters: Don't want to give up their individuality and become like everyone else. Assimilators: Don't want to stand out or look like they're troublemakers, want to get good grades. Adapters: Want to get along and show respect for the principal without completely losing their individuality, for example, wear one orange and blue article of clothing.)*

Ask class members: Which group do you think you would join? Why?

Tell students that in this chapter they will learn some of the ways the Jews responded to the challenge of maintaining their identities while under the control of a foreign ruler.

pages 16–17

Timeline

Invite students to read the timeline. Ask: Which timeline entry includes information about a popular Jewish holiday? *(164 BCE, Maccabees capture Jerusalem from Seleucids; Temple purified and rededicated)* What holiday is it? *(Ḥanukkah)* Invite students to share what they know about the holiday, in particular, the story of Ḥanukkah. Tell them that they will learn more about Ḥanukkah as they read this chapter.

page 19

You Are There: Resistance, Assimilation, or Adaptation

Before students respond to the questions in this activity, ask them to think back to the opening activity for the chapter, when they considered resisting, assimilating, or adapting in regard to the issue of the dress code. Ask: Did you have strong feelings about the position you took on that issue? Why or why not? How might you have felt if you had lived in Judea and had to choose an approach to Hellenism?

page 20

The Greek Torah: Septuagint

Ask for volunteers to debate the question "Should the entire synagogue Shabbat prayer service—including the Torah and *haftarah* readings—be conducted in

English?" Have one student or group of students represent the all-English position, another student or group represent the part-English/part-Hebrew position, and a third student or group represent the all-Hebrew position.

After each debater/group presents, invite the rest of the class to pose questions. (For example, students might ask the all-English group if they are concerned about the Jewish people losing their knowledge of Hebrew.) Finally, open the discussion for all students to share their personal points of view.

page 21 **Conflict in Judea**

Focus students on this passage: "Some of the younger priests neglected their Temple duties, preferring to take part in the neighboring athletic competitions." To help students understand how the tension between religious and secular commitments continues to this day, present this modern example: In 1965 the Los Angeles Dodgers were in the World Series and wanted Sandy Koufax, their ace pitcher, to start Game 1. But the game fell on Yom Kippur and Koufax decided to spend the day in synagogue.

Koufax did what he believed was the right thing; his manager and teammates supported him. But the day after the first game, Don Riley, a columnist for the *St. Paul Pioneer Press*, wrote a column that criticized Koufax for his decision. Some felt the column was antisemitic. Suddenly everyone was talking about the conflict of religion and sports.

Conduct a radio talk show on the subject with one student as the host, another as Sandy Koufax, and the rest of the students as listeners who call in. Alternatively, have students write a newspaper article or letter to the editor about Koufax's decision. Students may want to take the position of a sportswriter, rabbi, teammate, coach, Jewish fan, or non-Jewish fan.

You may want to suggest to students who are sports fans that they research information on Koufax and on Riley's editorial. (*Jewish Heroes, Jewish Values* [Behrman House, 1996] has a section on Koufax; see pages 12–15.)

page 21 **Map: The Diaspora During the Hellenistic Period**

Have students compare this map to a modern map of the Middle East. Ask: To which modern-day country does each arrow point? *(arrow pointing at Athens: Greece; at Perga and Edessa: Turkey; at Alexandria: Egypt)*

page 23 **Sound Familiar? Corruption in High Places**

Ask: What are some of the possible qualities that might be indications of a leader's trustworthiness? *(honesty, integrity, truthfulness, uprightness, reliability, sincerity, authenticity, and genuineness)*

page 24 **Ḥanukkah**

Remind students that there were no electric lights in the ancient Temple. The original menorah was at least the size of a person and gave off enough light to illuminate a very large room. (The Torah's instructions for creating the menorah are given in Exodus 25:31–40.)

You may want to take your students into the synagogue sanctuary and show them the *ner tamid* (eternal light) above the Holy Ark. Explain that all synagogues have a light above the Ark that remains lit twenty-four hours a day. These eternal lights are reminders of the menorah in the ancient Temple and of God's constant presence.

page 26 Photograph: Ancient Coin

After discussing the photograph on page 26, have students create coins for the modern State of Israel. Bring in strong aluminum foil and toothpicks and have the children etch the coins, or have them draw the coins using construction paper and markers or crayons. If you have some Israeli coins, bring them to class and use them to introduce the activity.

page 27 Then & Now

Possible answers to the first question: *There's so much commercial attention to and public celebration of Christmas that it can be difficult to resist the desire to join in; some families include people of different faiths; being different is not always given the consideration it deserves by others.*

Note: The issue of interfaith families can be a sensitive one. You may want to ask your rabbi or director of education to participate in this discussion.

Possible answers to the second question: *Learning about Jewish customs and traditions can help you make choices you feel good about. Make plans ahead of time that will help you celebrate Ḥanukkah in a fun way. For example, plan a latke party with a contest to see who can spin the dreidel the longest. Invite guests to bring latkes made of different foods—white potatoes, sweet potatoes, zucchini squash, turnips—even cheese!*

Family Connection

Have students discuss the "Then & Now" activity with their families. Invite them to share the ideas and points of view raised by their families. Alternatively, you may want to invite parents to join in the class discussion or to meet as a group with your rabbi or director of education.

3 Roman Domination of Judea

Divisions Inside and Out

textbook pages 28–39

Chapter Overview

A time of growing diversity and intolerance within the Jewish state was further complicated and aggravated by the oppression of Roman rule. Ideally, the Jews would have united against their common enemy. Instead, the tensions between the diverse groups (e.g., Sadducees, Pharisees, Zealots, and Sicarii) led to civil conflicts and the destruction of the Second Temple.

core concepts

- The Jews of Judea were diverse in their beliefs and practices.
- Their lack of tolerance and lack of respect for one another led them to the verge of self-destruction.
- Today we, too, are faced with the challenge of valuing what we Jews have in common with one another and tolerating our differences.

Learning Objectives

Students will be able to

- Explain how intolerance within the Jewish community helped bring our ancestors to the verge of destruction.
- Define the term *sinat ḥinam* (senseless hatred) and describe an instance of *sinat ḥinam* from ancient times and one from modern times.
- Apply what they have learned by suggesting at least one way in which our differences can strengthen the Jewish community today.

Teaching Opportunities

Getting Started

Relate the following Talmudic story (Babylonian Talmud, Gittin 55b–56a) to the class.

> A man whose friend was Kamtza and whose enemy was Bar Kamtza made a feast. He said to his servant, "Bring me Kamtza." But the servant mistakenly brought Bar Kamtza. When the host saw Bar Kamtza, he ordered him to leave. Bar Kamtza pleaded with the host for permission to stay, offering to pay for the entire feast just to be spared public humiliation. But the host threw him out, in full view of all the guests.
>
> Bar Kamtza thought, "The sages were present but did not protest. I will slander them to the emperor!"
>
> And, so, the Talmud tells us, Bar Kamtza went to the Roman emperor and slandered the Jews, reporting that the Jews were engaging in disloyal behavior. His words fueled the emperor's anger, leading him to send troops to attack and destroy Jerusalem and the Temple.

Ask: What might you have said to Bar Kamtza to persuade him not to go to the Romans? *(Express your hurt feelings to your community but remember the Jewish value of peace* [shalom] *and try to improve your relationship with your community.)* What might you have said to the host and guests who witnessed the injustice but made no effort to spare Bar Kamtza public embarrassment? *(There is no excuse for humiliating another person. Every human being is made in the image of God* [b'tzelem Elohim] *and should be treated with respect. Ask God and Bar Kamtza for forgiveness, and change your ways.)*

Explain that this story demonstrates the power of *sinat ḥinam,* or senseless hatred. Tell the class that in this chapter they will learn how intolerance brought our ancestors to the verge of destruction.

page 29 **Judea Divided**

Quickly review the concept of checks and balances that underlies the structure of the United States government in which each branch of government—executive, legislative, and judicial—can limit the power of the others. The Israelites had their own, more informal, system of checks and balances. While the king was the civil ruler and commander in chief of the army, the priests and prophets were the religious leaders of the community. Priests conducted sacrificial rites, and prophets instructed the people, including the king, in God's law. Some prophets were also counselors to the king, giving him political as well as spiritual advice.

Ask: What was the danger in the same person being both the king and the High Priest? *(He could have complete control over people's lives. He could use religion to gain political advantages. It would be harder for different points of view to be heard.)*

page 30 **The End of Independence**

To reinforce the concept of how the Jews' civil war caused them to disregard an external threat, invite students to talk or write about a time when a petty argument caused them to disregard an important issue. *(argument on the field between two teammates caused them to miss a ball and lose a game; competition between siblings caused an argument that ended up spoiling a holiday or birthday celebration)*

page 31 **Digging Up the Past**

Have students write a note to tell people two thousand years from now what their Jewish community was like. Invite students to focus on any aspects they choose, including how the community celebrates holidays and life-cycle events, conducts prayer services, organizes tzedakah projects, and runs its religious school. Students may want to include drawings of their synagogue and ritual items they have in their homes, such as Shabbat candlesticks, a seder plate, and a Ḥanukkah menorah.

To enrich the activity, you may have students create urns to hold their notes. You can use molding clay for pinch pots or decorate a small cardboard box or milk carton by gluing construction paper on the box and having students add decorations with crayons or highlighters.

page 32 **Famous Figures: Hillel and Shammai**

Explain that Hillel's summary of the Torah is a kind of motto that expresses an important Jewish value to live by. Give students five minutes to think about what their own personal life motto might be. Have students work independently and encourage them to consider what values their mottos express and what the values tell others about them. You may also want to ask in what ways their mottos express *Jewish* values. Invite each student to come to the front of the class, stand on one foot, and share his or her motto.

page 33 **Challenging the Romans**

After reading about how the Romans auctioned off the office of High Priest to the highest bidder, ask: What problems might arise when leaders are appointed based on who can pay the most for the position? *(doesn't require leaders to care about the people's needs or even know what their needs are; may lead to incompetent leadership)* Have students discuss how the auctioning off of the position of High Priest might be compared to today's wealthy politicians who are elected because they can spend the most on campaign advertising rather than because they have a strong track record and the skills to govern well.

page 34 **On the Brink of Rebellion**

Please note that the discussion of the Sicarii might disturb some students because they do not want to think of Jews as terrorists. You may want to consult with your director of education on the best way to present this material to your students.

page 34 **Map: The Revolt Against the Romans**

Ask: Where were the key Judean fortresses during the revolt in 66 CE? (*Gush Halav, Gamala, Yodefat, Sepphoris*) Where were the key fortresses during the revolt in 69–74 CE? (*Jerusalem, Herodium, Masada*)

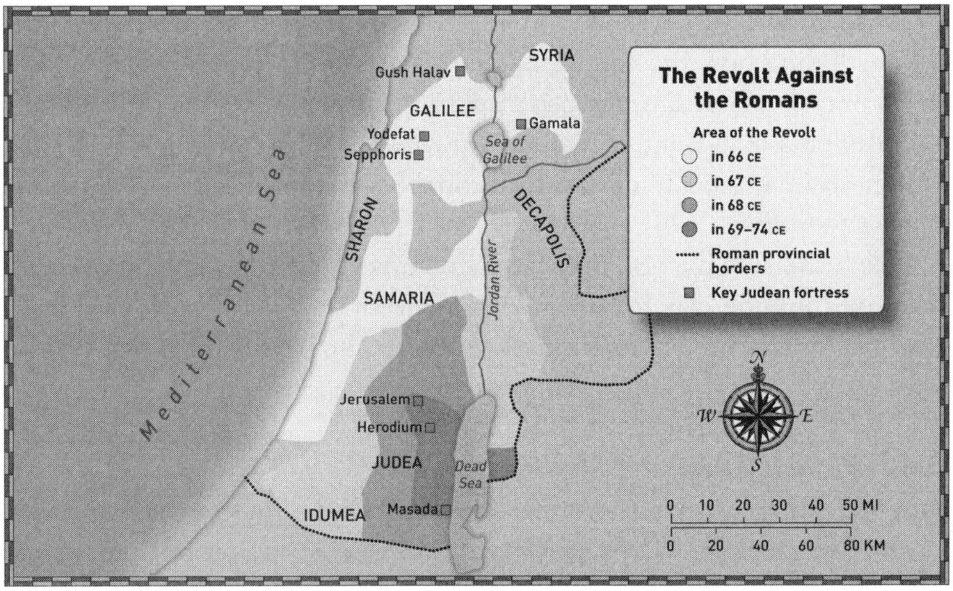

pages 35, 36 **Illustration: Josephus** and **The Jewish War**

After reading the photograph's caption and "The Jewish War" feature, invite students to compose a thought bubble for what Josephus was thinking in the illustration.

page 37 **Mourning for Jerusalem: Tisha B'Av**

Bring to class a calendar that includes Jewish dates and holidays and a Bible. Using the information in the feature, have students locate Tisha B'Av, the ninth of Av, on the calendar (July or August). Then help students to locate the Book of Lamentations in the Bible. (It is the sixth book in the Writings section of the Bible.)

Explain that Lamentations is a series of sad poems that tell of Jerusalem's destruction. In the poems Jerusalem is described as a woman. You might read aloud the opening verse of Lamentations:

> How the city sits alone
> That once was filled with people!
> She has become like a widow,
> She that was great among the nations.
> A princess among the other lands,
> Now she has become a slave

Have students identify the words that describe Jerusalem as a woman. Ask how this metaphor personalizes and intensifies the feeling of tragedy.

page 39 **Then & Now**

Ask: What are peaceful ways we can express political disagreement with others? *(conduct nonviolent demonstrations, write letters to elected officials, boycott goods, vote in political elections)*

Family Connection

Divide the class into several groups. Have each group create a short skit that dramatizes one or two sections of pages 34–38 in the textbook ("On the Brink of Rebellion," "The Revolt Begins," "War," "Jew Against Jew," "The Fall of Jerusalem," and "Last Stand at Massada").

Invite parents and other family members to come to a performance of these skits. After the performance conduct a discussion on the dangers of *sinat ḥinam,* senseless hatred, and ask for suggestions on what can strengthen the unity of your own Jewish community. *(greater tolerance of differences; more participation in community events, such as prayer services and holiday events; making an effort to socialize more with other congregants, e.g., inviting one another for holidays)*

You also may want students to perform their skits for other classes and invite your rabbi and director of education to participate in the discussions. At such events, consider taking photographs and offering them to your synagogue newsletter with a short article or placing the photos and article on your synagogue's Web site. Before posting photographs, check your synagogue's policy on gaining the permission of participants.

4 Rabbinic Judaism

Learning to Reinvent Ourselves

textbook pages 40–49

Chapter Overview

The most important adaptation during this period was shifting the center of Judaism from the Temple to the Torah. A key innovation was the establishment of an academy in Yavneh where Torah scholars could learn, debate, and pass on Jewish teachings from one generation to the next. The rabbis also established a religious court that decided which books would be included in the Bible and formalized aspects of prayer. Prayer eventually took the place of sacrifice, which had previously been the central form of Jewish worship.

core concepts

- The sages reoriented Judaism from a land-based cult religion to one that could survive and flourish after the destruction of the Temple and the exile of the Jews.
- Today we must continue to renew our vision of Judaism so that it not only survives the challenges of our own time but also thrives.

Learning Objectives

Students will be able to

- Describe a primary difference between Jewish life in Israel and the Diaspora.
- Identify one way the Jews communicated with God after the destruction of the Temple.
- Apply what they have learned in proposing ways in which they can maintain and strengthen their own Jewish identities.

Teaching Opportunities

Getting Started
Begin the lesson by asking students to name the different activities and places in the synagogue that help them to develop their identity as Jews, grow as Jews, and live as Jews. Have them explain their answers. *(religious school teaches Jewish values and how to read Hebrew, which helps them to grow and live as Jews and to participate in Jewish observance, such as prayer services; tzedakah projects help them put the mitzvah of giving to others into action; synagogue activities, such as Purim Carnivals, Shabbat dinners, and bar and bat mitzvah celebrations, bring them together with other Jews and make them feel like part of a community)*

Ask: How would your lives be different if there were no synagogue in our community? How would you learn to read Hebrew and pray? Where would you celebrate Rosh Hashanah or celebrate becoming a bar or bat mitzvah? What would be the center of our Jewish community?

Tell students that in this chapter they will learn how synagogues developed and became important in Jewish life.

pages 41, 43
Too Difficult to Bear
Explain that, over the centuries, Jews have wondered about God's role in the history of our people. In the time of the exile, many believed that God literally rewarded and punished the Jewish people—for example, by causing them to win or lose wars—in response to religious faithfulness or lack of faithfulness. Today, many Jews understand God's role in more abstract ways, for example, that belief in God can motivate us to find courage and strength when we are confronted by challenges.

page 43
Escape from Jerusalem
Rabbi Yoḥanan's escape led to the development of an important center of Jewish learning. This raises the issue of how one person can make a difference. Divide the class into collaborative learning groups of two to three students. Have each group prepare one example of a famous person who has made a difference in the lives of others and one of a less-well-known person who has made a difference in their school or community. Ask students to be ready to explain their choices. Then have the class come together to share their ideas. *(Examples may include people like Golda Meir, Martin Luther King Jr., the synagogue's cantor, a local politician, a classmate. Help students understand that a child raising money for the victims of a natural disaster, or participating in a coat drive in winter, or being a peer tutor in a literacy program, is also making a difference.)*

page 44 **Map: Synagogues in the Land of Israel, 1st–3rd Centuries CE**

You may choose to wait to review the map until the end of this chapter, after students have read about Hadrian, the second revolt, and the end of Jewish life in Judea.

Have students focus on the distribution of synagogue locations. Ask: What does this map suggest about the population of the Land of Israel from the first through third centuries CE? *(After the first century and the destruction of the Temple, Jews moved to the northern part of the land and built many more synagogues.)* Ask: What do you think would account for the move? *(Hadrian rebuilt Jerusalem as a Greek city and forbade the practice of Judaism, so the center of Jewish life moved north to cities and areas that had not been ravaged by war.)*

page 45 **Prayer House Plus**

For information on what the Judeans might be familiar with, focus students on the core text that begins on the last line of page 44 and continues on page 46: "Both in the Diaspora and in the Land of Israel, the role of the synagogue grew in importance.... Many early synagogues were a combination of prayer house, Jewish community center, and guest house. Synagogues held communal prayers and Torah readings. Some also hosted social activities, held classes for adults, and offered overnight accommodations for travelers."

Among the traditions and services that the Judeans would not have been familiar with are: *the practice of conducting bar and bat mitzvah ceremonies—bar mitzvah ceremonies did not exist until the Middle Ages and bat mitzvah ceremonies did not exist until more modern times—a religious school for children, and the inclusion of a pool and gym in a synagogue.*

page 46 **A Second Revolt**

Have students participate in this role-playing activity based on a fictional scenario: A woman from Tekoa, Tamar, has given refuge to her brother Etan who did not want to join Bar Kochba's army. Bar Kochba wants to burn her house down and force Etan, his sons, and her sons into his army. Bar Kochba wants to use this case to set an example for others who do not follow him. Etan and Tamar think he has no right to do this.

Assign volunteers to these roles: a judge, Bar Kochba, Tamar, and Etan. If you have a large class, you may want to include lawyers for Bar Kochba and Tamar, and Etan and Tamar's children. The remaining students can act as the jury.

Have both sides make opening arguments, examine and cross-examine witnesses, for example, Tamar, Etan, and Bar Kochba, then make closing statements. Finally, have the judge lead the jury in a discussion of who they think is right and why.

page 47 **Famous Figures: Babata**

The work of Israeli archaeologist Yigal Yadin gives us insight into what life was like for the rebels and their families. Among his most amazing finds were letters sent by Bar Kochba to the units under his command in Judea. In one, he requests that *lulavs* (palm branches) and *etrogs* (citrons) be sent to his soldiers so they might celebrate the holiday of Sukkot.

Have the class imagine: You are about to go to a faraway place with no access to Jewish sacred texts or ritual items, such as the Bible, a prayer book, a Kiddush cup, or Ḥanukkah menorah. Which three items would you most want to bring with you? Why?

page 49 **Then & Now**

Possible answer to first question: *Acts of loving-kindness including helping those in need.*

Possible answers to the second question: *Bring food donations to a shelter for the homeless; e-mail a friend who is ill; search the Internet for ways to help the needy, including people who have suffered a natural disaster.*

Family Connection

Invite students to explain to their families how synagogues grew in importance after the Holy Temple was destroyed. Ask the families how their synagogue helps them participate in Jewish life. Have students report back to the class on two ways in which the synagogue helps enrich their families' Jewish identities.

You may also have them suggest one innovation they would like to recommend to their synagogue and how they think it would benefit their family in particular and the Jewish community in general. For example, they might recommend that the synagogue offer a Hebrew class for parents of bar and bat mitzvah students. This would help them prepare for their children's celebration and also help increase the Hebrew skill level of the congregation as a whole.

5 Judaism and Christianity

The Parting of the Ways

textbook pages 50–61

Chapter Overview

At a time when there was much infighting among the Jews, corruption among the Jewish religious leadership, and oppression by the Roman rulers, the message of Jesus and his disciples offered hope to many disillusioned and poor Jews. Eventually, Judaism and Christianity split into two separate religions, followed by centuries in which there was much hostility, persecution, and mistrust between the two.

core concepts

- Christianity's roots are in Judaism.
- The seeds of mistrust, rivalry, and persecution were sewn in the process of Christianity becoming a separate religion.
- Improving interfaith relationships can help us make our world a better, more peaceful place.

Learning Objectives

Students will be able to

- Describe at least two traditions shared by Judaism and Christianity.
- Explain how both conflict among the Jews and conflict between Jews and Christians led to disaster.
- Apply what they have learned by recommending one action they can take to help improve relationships between Jews and Christians in their community.

Teaching Opportunities

Getting Started

Create two columns on the chalkboard. Label one "Similarities" and the other "Differences." Ask students who have siblings to describe two ways in which they are the same as or similar to their siblings and two ways in which they are different. Alternatively, to take into consideration those who don't have siblings, you may include comparisons to cousins or close friends. Write students' responses on the board under the appropriate columns.

Ask students how the similarities and differences make it easy or hard for them to get along with these family members and close friends. Encourage students to explain their answers. Ask students what they have done or can do to create more peaceful relationships when conflict arises.

Tell students that in this chapter they will learn how, in its early years, Christianity was part of the Jewish family, how it became a separate religion, and what happened to the relationship between Jews and Christians. Encourage students to continue to think about the relationships they just discussed as they try to understand the relationship between Jews and Christians.

Because they are surrounded by a Christian majority, many Jewish children are particularly interested in learning about Jesus and Christianity. You may want to give students paper on which to write their most pressing questions on these subjects. After reading this textbook chapter, and with the help of your rabbi and director of education, you should be able to satisfy students' curiosity.

Finally, throughout your discussions in this chapter and other chapters that cover the conflicts between Jews and Christians, it will be particularly important not to permit misinformation or prejudices to derail class discussions. Because some students may have Christian relatives, you will want to be especially sensitive to how these discussions are conducted.

page 51 A Longing for Change

Ask: Why might John have based a new ritual on an established and respected Jewish ritual? *(It probably felt comfortable and natural for John, who was Jewish and therefore familiar with the tradition of* mikveh. *Similarly, he might have preferred that the new ritual feel comfortable to the Jews whom he wanted to attract as followers.)*

page 52 Jesus of Nazareth

Ask students to list other aspects of Judaism and Christianity that are similar, in addition to believing in justice for the poor and abhorring greed. *(valuing peace and loving-kindness, a belief in one God, observing a Sabbath day of rest, honoring the Tanach—Torah, Books of Prophets, and Writings—as sacred text)*

page 54 **Seeking New Followers**

Make sure students understand that the Christian Bible is made up of the Hebrew Bible, or Tanach, and the New Testament. With the permission of your director of education, you may want to bring a Tanach and a Christian Bible to class to compare the table of contents of each. Note that the sequence of the books is different in each. For example, in the Tanach, the Book of Ruth and the Book of Chronicles 1 and 2 appear in the section called *Ketuvim*, or Writings, whereas in the Christian Bible they appear among the books of the Prophets.

pages 55, 57 **Shifting Blame**

After reading the last paragraph on page 57, have students once again consider their own relationships with family and close friends. Ask: What are the benefits of being tolerant and respectful of one another? How might this also apply to Jews and Christians?

page 56 **Famous Figures: Jesus of Nazareth**

Possible answers: *both taught people to love and honor God, pursue peace and justice, perform acts of loving-kindness, be compassionate; both offered hope for a better world.*

page 58 **Map: The Growth of Christianity in the Roman Empire, 1st–3rd Centuries CE**

Ask students to name the cities with the leading Christian communities. *(Alexandria, Antioch, Byzantium, Jerusalem, Rome)*

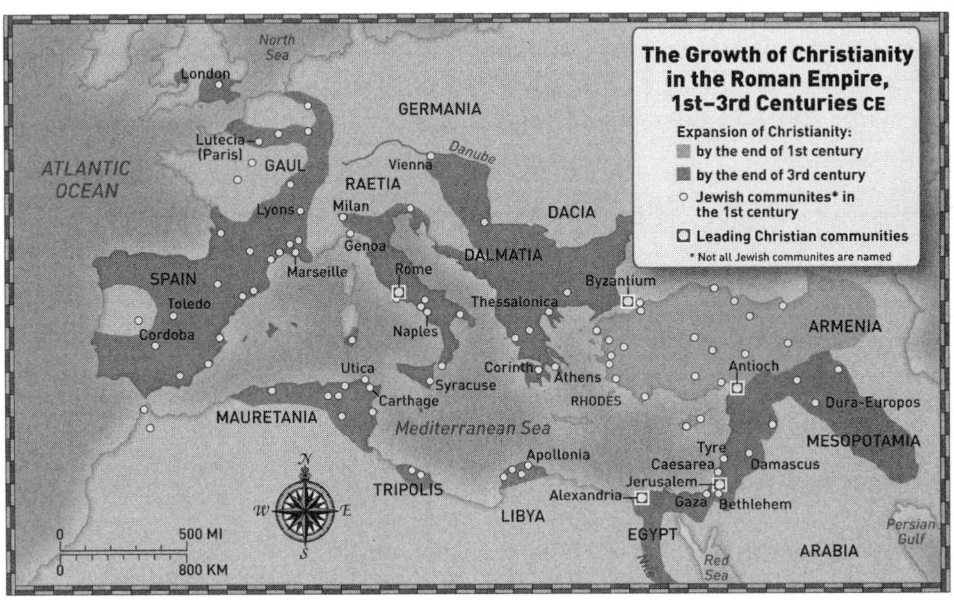

page 60 **Photograph: Memorial to Righteous Gentiles**

Ask students to research the Righteous Gentiles using your synagogue's library, the public library, or the Internet. Encourage them to learn about specific people, such as Raoul Wallenberg or Oskar Schindler, what they did, and the ways in which the Jewish people have sought to acknowledge and honor the Righteous Gentiles. Invite students to share their findings with the class.

page 61 **Then & Now**

Explain that prejudice is often borne of ignorance. Therefore, both teaching people about Judaism *and* learning about other religions can help add peace to the world. You may want to contact a local church to plan a joint event with your class and students in the same grade in their religious school. Before doing so, you may want to discuss the plan with your director of education and rabbi so that you best prepare your students for the event. You can choose a topic about which each group can share, for example, each group may teach the other about their Sabbath day observances or about a life-cycle or holiday event.

To emphasize the shared aspect of the two traditions, you may each want to teach a song whose words come from the Book of Psalms. Your cantor can guide you in selecting a song from the Jewish liturgy.

Begin by welcoming your guests and inviting everyone to introduce him- or herself. You can make the event more festive by serving light refreshments. If you serve refreshments, check what dietary regulations your synagogue observes and any dietary concerns your guests may have, including food allergies of students.

Family Connection

You can make the above activity a family affair by scheduling it at a time when family members can attend.

6 Babylonia

The New Center of Jewish Life

textbook pages 62–73

Chapter Overview

The growing importance of the Diaspora evolved as the Jews acclimated to Babylonian society. It also evolved as Jews were influenced by Babylonian culture and met the challenges of strengthening Jewish life. The Jews of this period not only developed the Babylonian Talmud, they also created a dynamic model for living as a minority in a non-Jewish environment.

core concepts

- After the destruction of the Second Temple, the Diaspora became the new center of Jewish Life.
- Judaism continued to evolve by adapting Jewish tradition to changing times and by integrating aspects of the surrounding cultures.
- To this day, the majority of Jews live outside of Israel and the Diaspora remains a central spiritual and creative force in Jewish life.

Learning Objectives

Students will be able to

- Identify challenges the Jews faced in Babylonia.
- Describe how our ancestors adapted to life in Babylonia.
- Apply what they have learned to explain how the Jews of Babylonia provided a model for strengthening Jewish life in the twenty-first-century Diaspora.

Teaching Opportunities

Getting Started

Say to students: Imagine that someone gave you a board game as a gift but when you opened the box there wasn't a detailed set of instructions inside. Ask: Without assistance, how would you know where to place the markers for each player, or when your turn came, or what was fair and what was cheating? Point out that it might be a great game but without a clear explanation of the rules, you couldn't play it.

Tell students that just as people need rules to play games, so, too, people need rules to successfully use the gift of life. Explain that the Torah offers such rules and instructions to the Jewish people, and that the Talmud—which was written by the ancient rabbis—provides more details and helps us apply the rules to our lives.

You may want to give students some specific examples of the relationship between the Bible and the Talmud. For example, Leviticus 19:14 teaches, "You shall not insult the deaf or place a stumbling block before the blind," but it is the Talmud that explains that this means that one should not mislead people or take advantage of them. Similarly, the Torah instructs us that on the holiday of Sukkot we should "live in booths for seven days" (Leviticus 23:42). But it is the Talmud that explains the specifics of how to build the booth, or *sukkah*: what materials to use, how high to build the walls, how many walls, and how to cover the roof.

Explain that the Talmud helped adapt Judaism to life in Babylonia and helped our ancestors maintain their Jewish identities. Tell students that the teachings of the Talmud continue to influence and guide many aspects of Jewish life today.

pages 62–63

Timeline

To help students preview the chapter, ask: Which timeline entry signals the beginning of a new world religion? *(570: Muhammad prophet of Islam, born in Mecca)* What is the name of the religion? *(Islam)* What is a follower of Islam called? *(a Muslim)* Invite students to share what they know about Islam, for example, the name of the holy book of Islam *(Koran)* and information they have learned through friendships with Muslims, the news media, and their studies in secular school.

pages 64–65

Next Step: The Talmud

Explain that in a traditional Talmud class, it is customary for students to study in pairs so that students can help each other understand the text and sharpen their thinking by challenging each other's ideas and logic.

Ask students if they generally prefer learning in small groups or large groups. Do they think that one of the two methods makes it easier for them to learn? Might they prefer a mixture of the two methods? What else helps them learn difficult subjects? (Keep students' answers in mind throughout the year. This information may give you valuable insight into students' learning styles and preferences.)

page 65

What Do You Think?

Help students understand that working and earning a living not only contribute to society but also help pay for food, clothing, shelter, and other basic needs a person has. Ask: What might happen if someone does not have the skills to earn a living and no family, friends, community, or government institution to help? *(person might become a thief/criminal)*

page 66

You Are There: Arriving in a New Land

Invite a foreign-born member of your congregation or of the larger community to speak about his or her experiences as an immigrant. In advance of the visit, have the class prepare questions for the guest on subjects such as why the person chose to emigrate, the person's first impressions of the people, climate, landscape, and way of life here, the difficulties of adjusting to a new way of life and language, and whether the person's attitudes and points of view have changed over time.

pages 67–69

The Challenge of Islam and The Roots of Islam

Ask: Why do you think the Muslims referred to Jews and Christians as "people of the book"? *(Because like the Jews and Christians, the Muslims accepted God as the source of the Tanach, or Bible)*

page 67

Map: The Growth of Islam, 7th–8th Centuries

Ask: What was the extent of Islam's growth? *(from Spain and Northern Africa to the Indus River)*

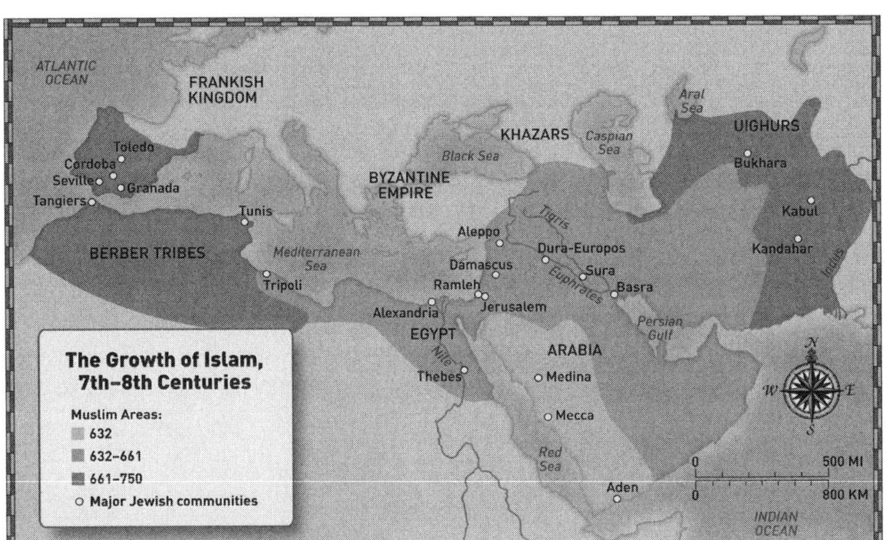

pages 69, 72 **Photograph: Three Girls** and **Photograph: Ruth Bader Ginsburg**

As a class, after discussing these photographs and their captions, have students research one or several modern North American Jews who have actively maintained their Jewish identities and also made valuable contributions to the society at large. (Students may do their research in the synagogue library or on the Internet.) Possible personalities to research include Lillian Wald, Joe Lieberman, Betty Friedan, Cynthia Ozick, Samuel Bronfman, Bella Abzug, Anne Roiphe, Steven Spielberg.

After completing their research, students can make oral presentations to the class. In addition, they can create bulletin board mini-posters by combining their written research with photos or drawings of the famous personalities.

page 71 **Chart**

Review the chart with your students. Ask them to consider what might have happened if the Babylonian Jews had not been able to adapt Judaism in the face of the challenges. Some possible answers include: *once the Jews were dispersed, without a standardized tradition, it would have been difficult to maintain a sense of unity and shared belief among the Jews; without laws that addressed real-life situations, Jews might have stopped seeking guidance from Judaism on how to live daily life; if the Jews had not translated the Bible and prayer book into a language they understood, Judaism's spiritual traditions might have been inaccessible or lost to most Jews; if the Jews had not broadened the types of knowledge and skills that were part of Jewish studies, many Jews might have rejected Judaism as old-fashioned and irrelevant to their lives; if the strengths of Judaism hadn't been highlighted, it would have been more difficult for Jews to see the benefits of maintaining their Jewish identities and more Jews might have sought to assimilate; if the Jewish leadership hadn't supported the importance of honoring civil laws, many Jews might have felt forced to abandon Judaism in order to continue to live in the Diaspora*

page 73 **Then & Now**

After completing the activity, invite students to think of ways in which they can integrate Jewish tradition into their celebration of a secular holiday. For example, they might want to recite the Sheheḥeyanu prayer before beginning their Thanksgiving meal or Independence Day barbeque.

Alternatively, encourage students to develop an innovation for an upcoming Jewish holiday. For example, explain that Ḥanukkah means "dedication" and suggest that students find an innovative way to rededicate themselves to Judaism on Ḥanukkah. One way could be for students to dedicate their Ḥanukkah *gelt*, or money, to an act of tzedakah, such as buying gloves and a scarf for a child in a homeless shelter, rather than on a present for themselves.

Family Connection

Invite students to explain to their families that much of Jewish history and religion existed as an oral tradition before it was written down and codified. Encourage students and their families to discuss their own oral traditions, especially those family stories that relate to Jewish life-cycle events, such as baby namings, weddings, bar and bat mitzvah celebrations, and to Jewish holidays and trips to Israel. Ask students to bring to class photographs and other objects that relate to these family stories and traditions. Invite students to talk about the items and to tell the stories that relate to them.

If you have access to a video recorder, you may want to tape-record students' presentations and invite families to view the tape and meet one another. If you hold such an event, take advantage of the community-building opportunity. Begin by welcoming your guests and inviting everyone to introduce him- or herself. You can make the event more festive and encourage people to socialize by serving light refreshments. If you do, check what dietary regulations your synagogue observes and any food allergies that may be an issue.

7 Sepharad and Ashkenaz

Judaism's Growing Diversity

textbook pages 74–85

Chapter Overview

Many Jews left Babylonia for what are now called Spain and Germany. The two groups became known, respectively, as the Sephardic and Ashkenazic communities. This chapter presents the diversity of the two communities, how each was influenced by the surrounding culture, and how each adapted Judaism to its new circumstances.

core concepts

- The Diaspora broadened when the Jews left Babylonia and settled in new places.
- Despite key shared traditions, such as the sanctity of the Torah and the Land of Israel, the Jewish communities in different geographic areas developed in distinctive ways.
- Today's Jewish communities are also diverse, even as we continue to share the same core traditions and values.

Learning Objectives

Students will be able to

- Identify primary differences between the Jewish communities of Spain and Germany.
- Describe challenges each community faced.
- Apply what they have learned to explain how these communities contributed to the diversity of today's Jewish world.

Teaching Opportunities

Getting Started

Explain that most Jews are descendants of those who lived in one of two geographic areas. Sephardic Jews are those whose families originated in Spain or Portugal, and Ashkenazim are Jews whose families originated in Germany or Eastern Europe.

Tell students that although the two communities have much in common—both celebrate Rosh Hashanah and Passover and, on Shabbat, both read from the Torah in synagogue—there are also differences between them. Present one or more examples of differences between the communities.

When possible, engage students' physical senses as well as their intellects. For instance, using a cookbook like *The New Jewish Holiday Cookbook* by Gloria Kaufer Greene (Times Books, 1999), prepare two different types of Passover ḥaroset for students to taste, one from each of the two communities. (If preparing the recipes is not possible, simply have students compare the ingredients, observing that the fruits that are used are quite different but that both recipes use fruit, wine, and nuts.)

In addition, or alternatively, invite your cantor to sing a piece of liturgy in two different styles, each reflecting one of the musical traditions. Or, with the help of your synagogue's librarian, select pictures of different ritual items, such as a seder plate, an *etrog* container, or a ḥallah cover, that show differences between the handcrafts of the Sephardic and Ashkenazic communities.

Encourage students to articulate the similarities and differences they observe. Then tell students that in this chapter they will learn about the origins of the Sephardic and Ashkenazic communities.

pages 75–79

The Golden Age of Spain

To illustrate the mixture of tensions and friendships between the Jews and Muslims, you may want to share the following story about Samuel Hanagid, who is discussed on pages 77–78 of the textbook:

> A story is told about Samuel Hanagid, an eleventh-century Jewish poet who was a close friend of the king of Spain, a Muslim. Jealous of the friendship between the two, a Muslim poet came before the king and falsely accused Samuel of stealing one of his poems.
>
> When told of the charges, Samuel showed the two men the many drafts of the poem that he had written. "All of my work is here for you to see how, step-by-step, I wrote and revised the poem."
>
> "And can you show me your drafts?" asked the king of the other poet.

"There are none," he sheepishly admitted.

"Then your punishment will be delivered by the hands of Samuel," declared the king. And turning to his friend, he continued, "Cut out this man's evil tongue, as he surely would have cut out yours."

Later that day the king passed the room of Samuel and heard the sounds of laughter. He opened the door and was surprised to find the two poets smiling and chatting.

"Samuel, this man is your enemy. Why have you not removed his evil tongue?" said the bewildered king.

"But I have, Your Majesty," Samuel replied. "I have removed his evil tongue and replaced it with a kind one."

page 76 **Map: Major Jewish Communities in the Islamic World, 8th–11th Centuries**

Name the major Jewish communities shown on the map. *(Jerusalem, Tiberias, Ramleh, Cairo, Damascus, Tripoli, Rome, Baghdad, Sana, Constantinople, Kairouan, Tiaret, Fez, Cordoba)*

Compare the map on page 76 to a modern map of the area. Have students locate the areas that were home to major Jewish communities and name the modern countries they are in. *(Israel, Egypt, Syria, Libya, Italy, Iraq, Yemen, Tunisia, Turkey, Algeria, Morocco, Spain)*

page 78 **The Golden Age of Spain**

The following excerpt is from the most famous poem by Judah Halevi. Although it was not created as liturgy, it is often included among the laments recited on Tisha B'Av, which mourns the destruction of the Holy Temple and Jerusalem.

> My heart is in the East and I am at the end of the West.
> How can I taste my food and how can I find pleasure in it?
> ...It would be easy for me to leave behind all the goodness of Spain,
> Just as, it would be glorious to see the dust of the Temple which lays in ruins....

After reading the excerpt aloud, ask students how they think Judah Halevi felt when he finally settled in Palestine. Ask why they think so.

page 80 **Famous Figures: Maimonides**

Maimonides defined eight levels of tzedakah, ordering them from the least to the most praiseworthy. The eight levels are listed on page 42 of this teaching guide. Write each level on the chalkboard but out of sequence. Challenge students, working individually or in teams, to put the list in the correct sequence by using logic to move from the least to the most praiseworthy. Have students present their choices and their reasoning to the class. You may want to hold a contest to see which student or team can be the first to put the levels in the correct sequence.

1. Giving reluctantly and with regret.
2. Giving graciously, but less than one should.
3. Giving what one should, but only after being asked.
4. Giving before being asked.
5. Giving without knowing the identity of the recipient, although the recipient knows the identity of the donor.
6. Giving anonymously.
7. Giving without knowing the identity of the recipient, and without the recipient knowing the identity of the donor.
8. Helping the recipient become self-supporting through a gift or a loan, or by finding employment for the recipient.

page 81 **Map: Ashkenazic Rabbinic Centers of Influence, 11th–13th Centuries**

Ask: Around which rivers did the Jews of Ashkenaz settle? *(Rhine, Loire, Seine, Meuse, Thames)*

Have students compare the map on page 81 to a modern map of the area. Ask them to locate the areas that were the Ashkenazic rabbinic centers in the eleventh to thirteenth centuries and to name the modern countries they are in. *(Great Britain, France, Germany, Switzerland, Czech Republic)*

pages 79, 81–84 **A Jewish Frontier Land**

After you have covered the section on the Jewish community leaders *(parnasim)* and independent board *(kahal)*, and the services they provided, invite a speaker from your local federation or other Jewish service organization to address your class. Have the guest speak about the organization's mission and work, for example, how the initiatives are divided between the Jewish community and services to the broader community. If possible, have the speaker discuss activities that the students and their families can participate in.

page 84 **Like Father, Like Daughter**

Explain that very few women had the educational opportunities enjoyed by Rashi's daughters. Girls from well-off families might receive a few years of education, but serious religious study was almost exclusively reserved for boys. As a result, most women could not speak or read Hebrew. In some learned or wealthy families, girls were sometimes given enough education to lead other women in prayers. On the thirteenth-century tombstone of Urania of Worms, for example, we read that she "officiated with a sweet voice before the women [in the synagogue]."

page 85 Then & Now

To enrich the activity you may want to invite a Sephardic member of the community or your rabbi to discuss some of the distinctive customs of Sephardic Jews. Alternatively, if your community is largely Sephardic, you may want to invite a speaker to discuss Ashkenazic customs.

Family Connection

You may want students to share the maps on pages 76 and 81 with their families. Have them ask if their families originated in any of these areas and invite them to share with the class the information they learn.

In addition, you may want to plan a Sephardic and Ashkenazic Food and Music Festival to which you invite students' families. You can provide the food or invite each family to bring in either a favorite recipe for a traditional Jewish food or to learn a new recipe. Make both Sephardic and Ashkenazic recipes available to families. Your synagogue librarian may be able to recommend Jewish cookbooks. Alternatively, you or the families can research recipes on the Internet. Be sure to check what dietary regulations your synagogue observes and inform families about them. Also let families know of any student allergies or other food concerns that are an issue.

Enlist the help of your cantor who may be willing to teach several songs from the Sephardic and Ashkenazic musical traditions or who can offer you an interesting selection of CDs.

Take advantage of the community-building opportunity. Begin by welcoming your guests and inviting everyone to introduce him- or herself. Then briefly describe the early history of the Sephardic and Ashkenazic communities or have students do so.

8 Medieval Europe

The Rise of Religious Persecution

textbook pages 86–97

Chapter Overview

The competition between Ashkenazic and Christian merchants led to restrictions that forced the Jews out of trade. Anti-Jewish laws were passed, many of which stripped Jews of their freedom and imposed high taxes. The increasing influence of the Catholic Church led to greater persecution of the Jews.

core concepts

- Due to religious prejudices, political factors, and economic competition, the Jews became targets of persecution and violence in medieval Europe.
- Today, many forms of prejudice plague our world. Because we have been the victims of persecution, we are particularly responsible to fight it.

Learning Objectives

Students will be able to

- Identify one primary cause of the persecution of the Jews in medieval Europe and the effect the persecution had on the Ashkenazic community.
- Describe how the Jews responded to the changing conditions and persecution.
- Apply what they have learned to explain why the experience and history of the Jewish people adds to our responsibility to help those who are oppressed.

Teaching Opportunities

Getting Started

Tell students that it is a Jewish tradition not only to study the history and stories of our people but also to use what we learn to guide our behavior in ways that both enrich our lives and help make the world a better place. That is why when we read the Passover story in the haggadah, we not only praise God for bringing us out of slavery in Egypt but *also* welcome those who are hungry to come and eat with us, and we consider how to help liberate those who are oppressed in our own day.

Explain that the Hebrew word *zachor,* meaning "remember," is often linked with taking action. For example, in the Ten Commandments it says: *Zachor et yom hashabbat lekadsho,* "Remember Shabbat and keep it holy" (Exodus 20:8).

Ask students how they think studying and remembering Jewish history can help guide their lives and actions. *(It can teach them how to maintain their Jewish identities and also participate in the secular world, build their relationships with the Land of Israel and be loyal citizens of the country in which they live, maintain their connections with other Jews even as they have business and social relationships with non-Jews, and help other Jews and other peoples who are oppressed.)*

Tell students that in this chapter they will learn about religious persecution against the Jews of Ashkenaz and consider how this knowledge can help guide their own lives.

pages 87–89

Warning Signals

Ask: If faced with similar circumstances today, what forums and resources do you think the Jews would have that they did not have in the eleventh century? *(United Nations, the modern State of Israel, politically influential Jews in North America, interfaith organizations)*

page 88

Map: Persecutions During the First Crusade

During the First Crusade, which communities were affected? *(Lynn, Rouen, Evreux, Metz, Trier, Mainz, Cologne, Rothenburg, Nuremberg, Regensburg, Prague)* In what direction did the crusaders travel in order to reach Palestine? *(east, southeast)*

pages 90–91, 93

Competition and Conflict

After students read the paragraph on page 91 that begins, "Laws were passed," write the following on the chalkboard: "A well regulated Militia, being necessary to the security of a free State, the right of the people to keep and bear Arms, shall not be infringed." Ask the class if anyone knows the origin of the quote.

Then write the following below the quote: The Bill of Rights Amendment II, 1791. (Explain that the Bill of Rights is the term for the first ten amendments to the United States Constitution. These amendments protect the rights of individuals by limiting the power of the federal government.)

Ask students why the freedom to bear arms was so essential to the Founding Fathers and why the prohibition was so dangerous for the Jews of medieval Europe. *(Angry mobs could rise up against the Jews at any time and Jews would not be able to defend themselves.)*

page 90 **Photograph: Life Vests**

After discussing the photograph and caption, invite students to think of other similes for the Jewish people's ability to adapt to new circumstances. For example, the Jews' ability to adapt to new circumstances is like a fountain of youth that keeps our people forever young. You may also want to have students create accompanying drawings.

page 90 **Chart**

Invite three volunteers to describe in their own words the impact of new technologies, how they affected Christians, and how that, in turn affected Jews.

page 92 **Famous Figures: Dolce of Worms**

To help students understand Judaism's emphasis on both the value of earning a living and the value of religious observance, share the following. The ancient sage Rabbi Eleazar ben Azaryah taught, "If there is no food, there is no Torah; if there is no Torah, there is no food (*Pirkei Avot* 3:17). In plain words this means that if our bellies are empty, we will be too hungry to concentrate on learning the lessons of Torah, but without the lessons of Torah, our lives will be without meaning and spiritual value.

Part of what made sages such as Rabbi Eleazar so wise was that they were realistic. They understood that if people do not earn a living so that they can have food and shelter, they will not survive. And if they do not survive, they cannot perform *mitzvot* (God's commandments). The Book of Psalms expresses this in a practical way: "The dead cannot praise God" (Psalm 115:17).

You may want to discuss with students how Judaism's balance between practical strategies and religious commitments has helped Jews and Judaism survive and thrive over the centuries.

page 92 **Famous Figures: Dolce of Worms**

Ask: Were you surprised to learn that there were successful women moneylenders in the twelfth century? Explain that the epitaph on Dolce of Worms's gravestone is similar to a section of the thirty-first proverb in the Bible's Book of Proverbs. This section of the proverb, Proverbs 31:10–31, is often called "Woman of Valor." It traditionally is recited by husbands to their wives on Friday nights. The poem praises the woman of the house.

You might read the entire poem aloud, or several verses, such as the following:

> She rises while it is yet night, and gives food to her household, and a portion to her maidservants (Proverbs 31:15).
>
> She considers a field and buys it; with the work of her hands she plants a vineyard (Proverbs 31:16).
>
> She generously gives to the poor and her hands are stretched out to those in need (Proverbs 31:20).
>
> She speaks with wisdom and the teaching of kindness is on her tongue (Proverbs 31:26).

Have students write a short essay or poem about their mothers or other strong women whom they admire, who exhibit some of the qualities listed above including being hardworking, generous, prosperous, kind, wise, caring, and multitaskers.

pages 93–95 The Jews Are Accused

After students read the paragraph on page 94 that describes the Catholic Church's order that Jews dress differently from Christians and wear special badges, ask: When in modern history were Jews forced to wear distinctive badges? *(During the Holocaust, Jews were forced to sew yellow stars of David on their clothing.)* Ask students why they think such actions would be humiliating and dangerous for Jews.

You may use this opportunity to continue your discussion of Righteous Gentiles, which began on page 60 of the textbook and page 33 of this teaching guide. Explain that during the Holocaust when the order for Jews to wear the yellow star of David was issued in Holland, 300,000 such stars were worn by the country's non-Jews. Each star proclaimed, "Jews and non-Jews stand united in their struggle." It is also reported that in Denmark, the law was never even ordered because King Christian X had warned that if there were such a law, he would wear the yellow star himself.

page 97 Then & Now

Before students work on this final activity, help them to understand that, depending on the circumstances and criteria, we all are in the minority at some point or other. To demonstrate this, conduct the following survey, and use volunteers to count and record the results on the chalkboard. Note how many children fit into each category: girl vs. boy; dark-haired vs. light-haired; owns a pet vs. does not; has lived at their current address for five years or more vs. for fewer than five years; plays a musical instrument vs. does not; loves strawberry ice cream vs. hates it.

You can create criteria that better suit your class. Keep in mind that the key concept for students to understand is that at some point we are all members of a minority group.

Family Connection

Point out that over the centuries the Jewish people have traveled from country to country looking for safe and welcoming homes. In fact, because of persecution and economic difficulties, some families have stayed in a country for only a few years or for a generation or two before moving on to the next place.

Invite students and their families to create family trees that not only indicate who the members of each generation were but also their countries of origin. Have students share their family trees, perhaps even decorate them. In addition, invite students to bring in and share photographs of people and photographs or drawings of items—such as Shabbat candlesticks, old passports, and articles of clothing—they may have from a time when their families lived elsewhere. Discourage children from bringing in actual artifacts, such as family heirlooms or other valuable items, that can be damaged or lost.

9 The Sephardic Diaspora

Rebuilding Jewish Life

textbook pages 98–109

Chapter Overview

As a result of their expulsion from Spain, Sephardic families spread out in many directions, building new Jewish communities from Asia to the Americas. They enriched Judaism with works on Jewish law, such as Rabbi Joseph Caro's Shulḥan Aruch, with the development of the Ladino language (the Sephardic equivalent of Yiddish), and by creating the foundation of a Jewish community in North America. This was also a period of upheaval, a period when, in their search for hope, many Jews were taken in by false messiahs, such as Shabbetai Zevi.

core concepts

As a result of the Sephardic community's expulsion from Spain, Jews learned to

- Never take their security for granted.
- Value the ties that unite all Jews no matter what their differences.
- Be flexible and adaptable.

Learning Objectives

Students will be able to

- Explain why the Jews were expelled from Spain.
- Describe how the Sephardic Jews adapted to their new countries.
- Apply what they have learned to explain how the experience and contributions of the early Sephardic Diaspora continues to influence us today.

Teaching Opportunities

Getting Started

Ask students what kinds of secrets they sometimes have to keep. *(Possible answers: kept a secret about a surprise party, a birthday gift, personal information that a friend had confided)* Have students share their experiences and discuss their feelings about not being able to be completely open and honest with others. Focus students on the pressure they may have felt to not slip up and divulge the secret.

Now invite students to list some of their favorite hobbies and interests, such as playing soccer, the piano, and video games. Record their responses on the chalkboard. Ask: How might you feel if one day you were forbidden to engage in these activities ever again? What would you do if the consequence of engaging in them was that you and your family would be shunned by everyone in town and possibly arrested? If you really loved the activity, might you continue to engage in it in secret? Would you seek to move away? What if other towns in your area started to make the same rule?

Tell students that in this chapter, they will learn about the threats the Jews of Spain faced to their ability to live as Jews and how they overcame the challenge.

page 98 **The Big Picture**

After reading "The Big Picture" as a class, individually, or in small groups, invite students to discuss their thoughts and feelings on learning that in 1492 Queen Isabella, who sponsored the journey that led Christopher Columbus to the Americas, also issued—with King Ferdinand—an order expelling all Jews from Spain. Students may need a moment to reflect on the overlap of this famous world event with a piece of Jewish history.

pages 99–100 **Secret Jews Go Underground** and **The Jews Are Expelled**

After reading the sections as a class, individually, or in small groups, review the meanings of *conversos*, crypto-Jews, and *marranos*, helping students to distinguish between the three terms: *Conversos* were Spanish Jews whose lives were spared in the late 1300's when they converted to Christianity. Crypto-Jews, or secret Jews, were *conversos* who continued to practice Judaism in secret. *Marranos* is a Spanish word meaning "swine"; it is the derogatory name given to Sephardic Jews who were suspected of being secret Jews.

page 100 **The Jews Are Expelled**

Have students write perspective journals from the viewpoint of a Sephardic Jew living in Spain in 1492. Ask them to choose one of the following roles: a child, an adult, or an elderly person, indicating whether they are male or female. In their journals, have students describe whether they plan to become *conversos*, live as crypto-Jews, or remain Jewish and leave Spain. Ask them to also describe the issues that influenced their decisions, such as concerns about family, financial and professional issues, ties to the Jewish community, emotional, cultural, and spiritual ties to Judaism, ties to Spain, and knowledge or lack of knowledge of languages other than Spanish. Invite students to read their journals aloud to the class.

pages 100, 102 **Searching for a Place to Live**

Ask: Do you think that given our history of needing refuge from persecution and oppression, Jews should be particularly responsible to reach out to refugees from other countries? (You may want to point out that Jews have suffered persecution as recently as the Holocaust and in places as far-flung as Argentina, Syria, Iran, and the former Soviet Union.)

To link the discussion with a social action project, talk about a contemporary refugee problem that is in the news and, as a class, research opportunities to help, such as writing letters to politicians and collecting money to provide aid.

page 102 **Map: Sephardic Communities in the Diaspora**

Ask: Which were the two longest distances and the two shortest distances Sephardic Jews traveled to find new homes? *(Longest: Mexico City, Lima; Shortest: Algiers, Tangiers)*

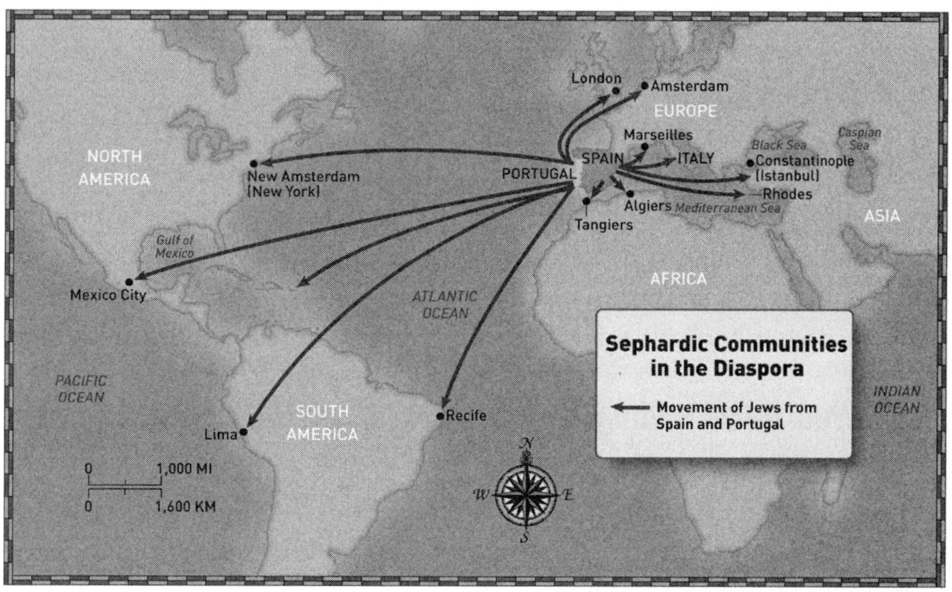

page 103 **Famous Figures: Doña Gracia Nasi**

Possible answers: *Jews like Doña Gracia Nasi are willing to risk their lives to remain Jewish because of their deep religious belief. They believe it is their sacred duty to remain Jewish. They believe they are honoring God by remaining Jewish.*

page 104 **Ladino: A New Language of Our Own**

Invite the cantor to sing and teach several Ladino songs or share Ladino CD recordings. If possible, include both liturgical and secular music. Compare several Ladino liturgical melodies with Ashkenazic melodies for the same prayers.

If you have students who play musical instruments or sing, you may want to ask volunteers to learn and perform a Ladino song. Speak to your cantor who might want to include such student performances as part of a synagogue prayer service, or speak with your director of education who might want to include it as part of a religious school prayer service. In addition or alternatively, you might ask for volunteers to research information on musical instruments that are used to perform Ladino music. Invite the volunteers to present their findings to the class.

page 104 **The Long Road to New York**

Contact your local historical society or use other resources to find out when the first Jews arrived in your community and where they came from. You may also want to research some of the other Jewish firsts in your area, such as the first synagogue, kosher butcher, Jewish community center, and Jewish religious school.

page 105 **Repairing the World**

Many mystics continue to be drawn to the city of Safed today, making pilgrimages to visit the grave of Rabbi Isaac Luria who is buried there. Safed is also well-known for its many art galleries. If students have been to Safed or have family members who have been there, invite them to share photographs of and stories about their visit.

pages 105–107 **Following False Messiahs**

Many question whether Shabbetai Zevi was a fraud or a madman. Some think he may have suffered from manic depression. Although there is no way to know for certain, this diagnosis conforms to anecdotal accounts and biographical details that describe Shabbetai Zevi as having alternating bouts of exultation and depression.

pages 107, 108 **Say What You Think, Photograph: Spinoza,** and **What Do You Think?**

Ask for volunteers to debate the question of whether or not Spinoza should have been excommunicated. Have one student or group of students represent the pro-excommunication position and another student or group represent the anti-excommunication position. After each debater or group presents its position, invite the rest of the class to question them. For example, students might ask the anti-excommunication person or group what actions they would have taken to prevent negative consequences arising from Spinoza's influence. Finally, open the discussion for all students to share their personal points of view.

page 109

Then & Now

Using index cards or sheets of writing paper, you may have students fill out pledge cards in which they promise to fulfill at least one mitzvah of *tikun olam* (for example, visiting the sick, helping the poor, or doing peer tutoring) within a specific time, such as in the following week or month. The template for the card might read: I (student's name) do hereby promise to fulfill the following act of *tikun olam* (describe the action to be taken) by (date by which it will be done). Ask students to fill in the blank lines on the pledge cards and then sign and date them.

Ask students to record in their notebooks the mitzvah they pledged to fulfill and the date by when they will fulfill it. Collect the signed pledge cards. At the appropriate time, ask students to share the experience of what they did and how it helps repair the world. *(sample response: visited sick friend and thereby helped repair the world by adding compassion to it)*

Family Connection

As an alternative to the above activity, or in addition to it, have students and their families pledge to perform acts of *tikun olam* within the family or in the community. Invite students to share what their families did and how such actions help repair the world. Students may also write up and illustrate their experiences to help create a *tikun olam* bulletin board.

10 The Polish Kehillah and German Enlightenment

Models of Isolation and Integration

textbook pages 110–121

Chapter Overview

The ghettoes of Poland and Lithuania segregated the Jews from their neighbors. The Jewish Enlightenment *(Haskalah)* paved the way for Jews to become integrated into modern society. It made it possible for Jews to live and work with their non-Jewish neighbors.

core concepts

- Judaism has often straddled the line between isolation and integration—maintaining close ties within the Jewish community and interacting with the broader community.
- Both approaches have helped to enrich Judaism and led to diversity.

Learning Objectives

Students will be able to

- Describe how circumstances in Eastern Europe caused Jewish life to become more diversified.
- Explain why Jews started to become more involved in the larger secular community.
- Apply what they have learned to identify similarities and differences between the eighteenth- and nineteenth-century Jews of Poland and Lithuania and their own Jewish communities.

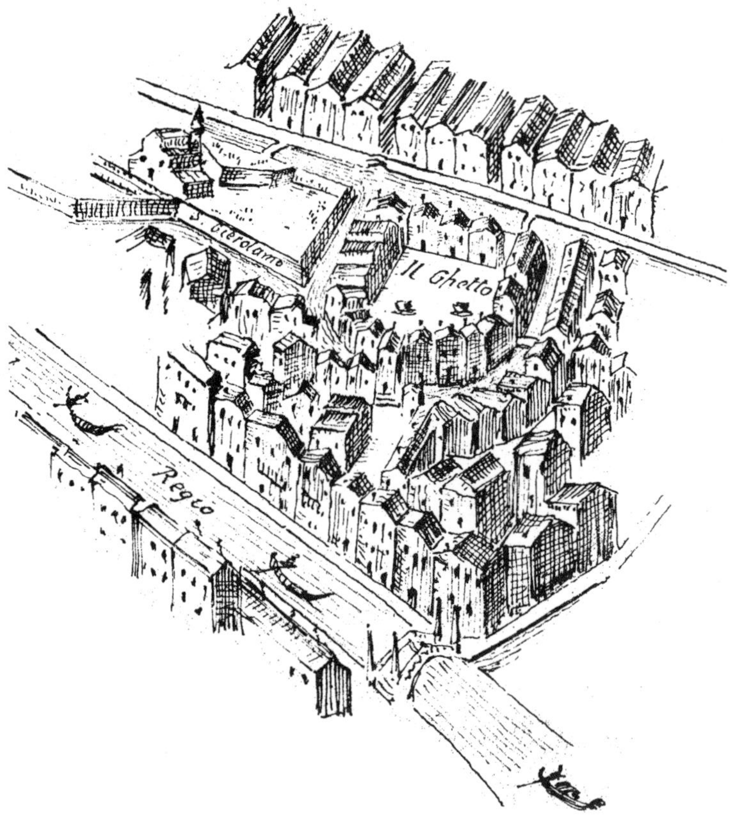

Teaching Opportunities

Getting Started

Begin this lesson by familiarizing students with Yiddish. Explain that Yiddish is a mixture of Hebrew, Aramaic, and German, and first developed in Germany. Over time, Yiddish also has incorporated numerous words from the languages of other lands where Ashkenazic Jews have lived. Although only a small minority of today's Jews speak Yiddish, less than a century ago more than half the Jews in the world spoke Yiddish, many as their primary language.

Listed below are several ways to provide students with a taste of Yiddish.

1. If a member of your community is fluent in Yiddish, you may want to invite him or her to introduce the language to your class and teach students a few phrases. You or the speaker might teach words such as *shul* (synagogue), *yarmulke* (skullcap, or *kippah* in Hebrew), and *mensch* (an honorable, decent person). You can point out that many Yiddish and Hebrew words are the same but are pronounced differently. For example, both *mazel tov* (Yiddish) and *mazal tov* (Hebrew) mean "congratulations," and both Shabbos (Yiddish) and Shabbat (Hebrew) refer to the seventh day of the week. You might also point out that some Yiddish words, such as bagel and nosh, have been integrated into English. Invite students to share Yiddish words they know.
2. Tell students that written Yiddish uses Hebrew letters. If you like, divide your class into teams and do a timed activity in which each team is given a copy of the same paragraph or page in Yiddish. Have students identify letters they know from Hebrew. The first team to find twelve letters they recognize wins. (Students must point to each letter they recognize and name its Hebrew look-alike.)
3. With the help of your synagogue librarian or cantor, locate Yiddish folk music to play for students. Your cantor may also want to teach students one or two songs in Yiddish.

Tell students that in this chapter they will learn about the Jews of Eastern Europe who spoke Yiddish as their main language.

pages 111, 113

Living Apart

Before students read the text on page 111, ask them what the benefits are of having a religious school and synagogue in their community. *(provides a place where they can learn about Judaism, provides professionals to lead the community, provides a place to celebrate holidays and life-cycle events with the community and to pray, provides a place where Jews who move to the neighborhood can find friends and develop ties with the community)*

Ask: What might be a benefit of all Jews being *required* to be members of a synagogue and religious school community? *(More people would share in the expenses; it might strengthen the Jewish identity of Jews who might not otherwise feel connected to Judaism; more people might decide to study Judaism.)*

Ask: What might be some of the drawbacks of all Jews being required to join a synagogue and religious school community? *(Some Jews might resent being forced to join the community and be angry; it might force all Jews to live in the same area in order to be close to the synagogue and religious school; Jews might start seeing non-Jews as outsiders.)*

After discussing the above questions, read the "Living Apart" section as a class or in small groups. Ask students how living in an all-Jewish neighborhood *(shtetl)* and speaking a special Jewish language (Yiddish) might have strengthened Jewish life.

page 114 Sound Familiar: Jewish Self-Government

Possible responses: *Being self-governing helped the Jews maintain and strengthen their identities as Jews, strengthened the Jews' sense of community and unity, helped the Jews feel safer than they did when relying on non-Jews to look after their interests.*

page 114 Map: Major Jewish Communities of Poland, 17th–18th Centuries

Provide a modern map and ask: In what countries in today's Europe may the major Jewish communities on this map be found? *(Poland, Germany, Ukraine, Belarus, Lithuania, Latvia)*

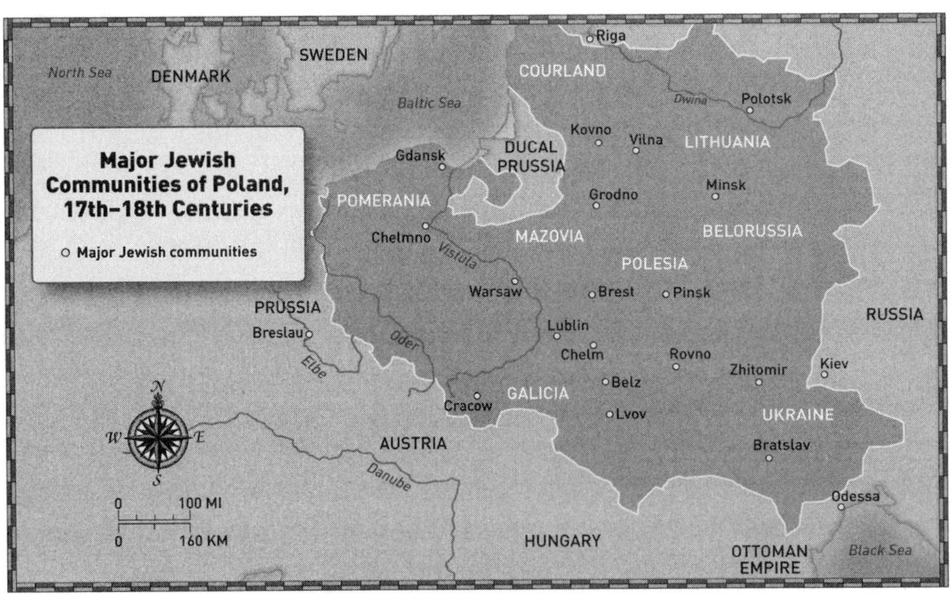

page 116 **Ḥasidic Tales**

Have students read this feature after completing the "Jews with Different Views" section on pages 115–18. Possible responses to the first question: *Many followers lived difficult and impoverished lives; this story acknowledges that when you are concerned about basics, such as food and shelter, life is especially challenging. Given that many of the followers felt powerless in the face of wealthy Jewish community leaders (whom they may have perceived as living in heaven), the story may have made them feel better about themselves by acknowledging that life is especially hard when you are poor.*

page 117 **Techines: Personal Prayers**

Ask the professional who leads prayer services at your school if a selection of students' prayers can be included in an upcoming school prayer service. If they can be, invite students to volunteer to read their prayers at the service.

pages 118, 120 **"Dare to Know!"**

Have volunteers read one paragraph each in the textbook. After reading Immanuel Kant's quote, "Dare to know!" ask: Why might it take daring and courage to learn? *(Learning new ideas may make us question old beliefs and relationships; it may make us change our beliefs and behaviors.)*

page 119 **Famous Figures: Moses Mendelssohn**

Invite students to discuss or debate whether or not it is easier to maintain and strengthen one's Jewish identity in an open society where one is free to study, think, and say whatever one wants, than it is in a closed society.

page 120 **Chart: Three Adaptations to Life in Poland and Lithuania**

Invite three volunteers to each read one of the three points of view. Then invite students to express their own points of view about what is most important about living as a Jew in today's world.

page 120 **Change Is in the Air**

Divide your class into three groups representing *Ḥasidim*, *Mitnagdim*, and *Maskilim*. Ask each group to write a short speech to be presented at a *brit milah* (circumcision) ceremony. Ask each group to extend wishes for the child that express what its community values most.

The *Ḥasidim* might emphasize the child spreading love of God through joy, song, and dance, especially as expressed in prayer; the *mitnagdim* might speak of their hope that the infant grows up to become a religious scholar deeply committed to the study of Talmud and to carefully following the *mitzvot*, and the *maskilim* might express their hope that the boy becomes learned in secular fields as well as Judaic studies, that he makes choices that add meaning and strength to his life as well as to the community.

After students have written their speeches, invite them to present them to the class. You may want to serve grape juice and cookies or fruit to make the occasion more festive and lively. As always, when serving food, check what dietary regulations your synagogue observes and any dietary concerns students may have, including food allergies.

page 121

Then & Now

The areas about which students may seek to interview others could include holiday and life-cycle observance, such as Ḥanukkah, Passover, weddings, and bar and bat mitzvah celebrations. It also might include their interest in synagogue membership, knowledge of Hebrew, Ladino, or Yiddish, and experiences visiting Israel.

Family Connection

Create a chart of all the Yiddish words students know. Invite students to interview their parents and other relatives, as well as family friends, in order to collect additional words and phrases. (Remind students that names of foods, such as *kugel* and *cholent,* count!) Invite students to bring in the list of words to class. You may then want to create a class dictionary of Yiddish words. Encourage students to begin to pepper their English with Yiddish words.

If you have students whose families know Ladino, you may want them to share Ladino words and phrases with the class and create a separate Ladino dictionary.

11 Revolution and Emancipation

The Challenge of Freedom

textbook pages 122–131

Chapter Overview

Before emancipation, Jews often were forced to live separately from their non-Jewish neighbors. In addition, they were pressured by their leaders and peers to follow Jewish law and tradition. The American and French Revolutions brought freedom to the Jews and resulted in increased assimilation. As the ideas and spirit of the American and French Revolutions spread through Western Europe, including Belgium, Holland, England, and Germany, so did emancipation. In Poland and Russia life improved for the Jews but emancipation did not come until the twentieth century.

core concepts

- After emancipation, Jews no longer were required to be members of the Jewish community or to participate in Jewish communal life. Both issues became matters of personal choice.
- In modern democratic countries we continue to identify and to choose to live as Jews, and this fact continues to shape Judaism.

Learning Objectives

Students will be able to

- Describe the opportunities emancipation afforded the average Jew.
- Identify the challenges that came with this increased freedom.
- Apply what they have learned to explain how these challenges continue to affect our lives today.

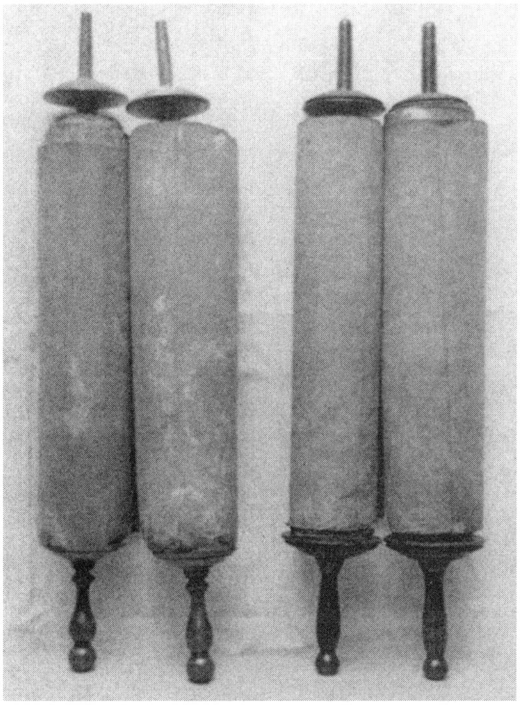

Teaching Opportunities

Getting Started

Invite students to share the key facts of the American Revolution. Establish that the colonists objected to British policies, in particular the heavy taxes the British imposed on them, and that the Continental Congress declared independence in 1776. The Revolutionary War ended when a peace treaty recognizing the independence of the American colonies was signed in 1783.

Invite students to name some of the leading figures of the American Revolution. *(George Washington, Thomas Jefferson, Benjamin Franklin, Thomas Paine)* Ask: Do you know who Haym Salomon was? Explain that Salomon was a Jew who lived in New York City during the American Revolution. Tell students that in this chapter they will learn about Salomon's role in the revolution and how the Jews were affected by the revolution and its aftermath.

pages 123–125

Freedom's Call

In 1654, Peter Stuyvesant, the director-general of New Amsterdam, reluctantly permitted the Jews to settle in his town. The Jews, he claimed, were "deceitful" and "hateful enemies and blasphemers of the name of Christ." More than four centuries later, Jews have integrated into and contributed to the life of New York in every way—as mayors, senators, artists, scientists, educators, clothing manufacturers, architects, police officers, firefighters, and much more.

The "Family Connection" activity on page 62 suggests that students discuss, with their families, relatives who have immigrated and made contributions to their communities through their work, volunteer activities, charitable acts, or military service. You may want to assign the activity at the beginning of the chapter, encouraging students to interview a relative who immigrated or who remembers immigrant relatives and their contributions. Have students share with the class their findings as well as photographs and other memorabilia that their parents permit them to bring to school.

page 124

Map: Major Jewish Communities in the Americas, 1750

Ask: Where were the Jews of the New World located? *(Caribbean, northern South America, and the Eastern Seaboard of North America)* Why do you think all the early significant Jewish communities in North America were located on the Eastern Seaboard? *(They were living in the thirteen colonies, along with the majority of European settlers—this was before the American Revolution in 1776.)*

page 124 **Photograph: Torah Scrolls**

Explain to students that, although Torah scrolls may be dressed in different protective coverings, all scrolls have the same exact words and are written in the same way. In other words, the Torah scrolls that the early Jewish-American colonists read at prayer services were exactly the same as the ones they had read in Europe and as the ones we read today. So, too, the Bible stories read and studied by the settlers and by their grandparents, great-grandparents, and the many generations before them in countries around the world are the same stories we read and study today.

page 125 **Haym Salomon**

Some possible answers: *Causes that might be important to students include: feeding and clothing the homeless, protecting the environment and animal life, supporting Israel. Students can donate books and toys to shelters, run coat drives and bake sales, volunteer their time, recycle, donate money to animal shelters, write letters in support of Israel to politicians.*

page 126 **A Symbol of Freedom**

Answer: *The words on the proposed seal mean that when we fight against tyrants and dictators we are following God's teaching that people should be free from oppression.*

page 126 **Photograph: U.S. Postage Stamp**

Discuss the photograph and caption. Ask: Do you think the stamp violates the separation of church and state? Would your view be different if the Ḥanukkah postage stamp were the only stamp that one was permitted to use in December? Are there certain religious images that you think should never appear on a stamp? Encourage students to explain their responses.

page 128 **Freedom Brings New Challenges**

Explain that the phrase, "To the Jews as a nation, nothing; to the Jews as individuals, everything" summarizes the shift that emancipation brought. No longer was the status of Jews based on their being members of a particular religious group, but rather on their status as individual citizens.

page 128 **Emancipation Spreads**

Invite students to write a perspective journal entry from the point of view of a teenage member of the Belgian Jewish community when emancipation is announced. Have students describe what they look forward to as a result of emancipation, as well as what they are concerned about.

page 129 **You Are There: Napoleon's Questions**

Help students understand that, in the activity, the contrast of "relatives" and "strangers" refers to Jews being willing to identify themselves as French nationals rather than as outsiders.

page 130 **Famous Figures: Grace Aguilar**

After students have read the feature, ask: Do you agree with Grace Aguilar that women should be taught to understand Jewish values and observances, not simply trained to accept them? Why or why not? Do you think the same is true of men? Why or why not?

Possible answers to the activity question: *Because crypto-Jews were not easily able to study Judaism, Aguilar thought Jewish education was particularly precious. Because education was not easily available to crypto-Jews, many had a limited understanding of Jewish tradition and history. Aguilar may have thought that crypto-Jews' lack of knowledge jeopardized their ability to keep the tradition alive and pass it on to the next generation.*

page 131 **Then & Now**

Possible answers to the last question: *Maintaining Jewish identity gives one a sense of being part of a long and sacred tradition; gives one a sense of purpose, for example, to pursue justice and work for a more peaceful world; gives one a sense of belonging, especially when one joins a synagogue and other communal organizations; provides a tradition for developing one's spiritual life; provides guidance in how to live a fulfilling life.*

Family Connection

Invite students to share information on Haym Salomon with their parents. Encourage students and their families to talk about relatives who have immigrated to this country and who have contributed to their communities and country as a whole. Point out that there are many ways to contribute including through the work one does, volunteer activities and charitable acts one performs, and serving in the military. Have students share their findings with the class as well as photographs and other memorabilia that their parents permit them to bring to school.

12 Judaism and the Modern World

Finding a Balance

textbook pages 132–143

Chapter Overview

Jews entered the middle class in major cities in England, Germany, Russia, and Poland, where they were encouraged to assimilate. They struggled to adapt Judaism and Jewish identity to the modern world. This fostered the rise of Reform Judaism, ultra-Orthodoxy, and the forerunners of Conservative Judaism and Modern Orthodoxy.

core concepts

- In order to maintain their Jewish identities, emancipated Jews either had to reject modern culture or had to adapt Judaism. Their choices led to greater diversity.
- We face similar challenges and similar opportunities today.

Learning Objectives

Students will be able to

- Explain how changes in the modern world influenced the Jews.
- List at least two adaptations that were made to Judaism.
- Apply what they have learned to describe at least one way in which adaptations to Judaism continue to be made today.

Teaching Opportunities

Getting Started

Using a piece of self-sticking paper, such as large name tags, have each student write two Passover seder traditions that he or she thinks should always remain the same, such as eating matzah and reciting the Four Questions, and two traditions that he or she would want to adapt or add to the seder, such as adapting the Cup of Miriam by filling it with sugar water to symbolize the sweetness of freedom's path and adding a pomegranate to the seder plate, its many seeds symbolizing the diversity of the Jewish people in Israel and the Diaspora. Ask students to be prepared to share their reasons for each choice.

Have students attach the self-sticking notes to their shirts and walk around the room reading each other's choices. After reading all the notes, ask them to each select a partner who has made at least one choice that is different from theirs. Working with their partners, invite students to discuss their choices and reasons for five to ten minutes.

Ask the partners to negotiate a common set of four choices. Then reconvene as a class, inviting the partners to share their ideas about maintaining and changing the seder traditions and their reasons. Encourage students to discuss their experience of negotiating a common set of choices and also point out the diverse choices within the class.

Explain that in this chapter students will learn how the Jews of Europe adapted Judaism to changing times and circumstances, increasing the diversity of the Jewish community.

pages 133–134

Jews Join the Middle Class

After reading the text as a class, in small groups, or individually, say: Imagine that you are living in Germany in 1870. Of all the changes that are described in the passage you just read, such as changing one's style of dress, no longer speaking Yiddish, and studying secular subjects, which is most difficult for you to make? Why? Which do you think is the most important change for you to make? Why? Is there any change that you would refuse to make? Why?

Students may discuss these questions in small groups and then share their thinking with the class, or this may be conducted as a class discussion.

page 135

Famous Figures: Moses Montefiore

After completing the writing activity, arrange students in a circle and ask them to complete this sentence: Helping Jews in other countries can strengthen my Jewish identity by… *(teaching me about other Jewish communities, building bridges between me and other Jews, strengthening my ties to Israel, enabling me to perform the mitzvah of tzedakah, reminding me that I am part of a tradition that is practiced around the world)* Remind students that even as they reach out to Jews in other countries they can continue to be responsive to the needs of Jews in this country as well as to the needs of non-Jews.

page 136 **Photograph: Heinrich Heine**

Explanation of the meaning of baptism as a "ticket of admission to European culture": *By converting to Christianity (becoming baptized) Heine believed he would be well received in high-level European social and professional circles.*

pages 134, 136 **Two Different Experiences**

After reading the text, write the following Heine quote on the blackboard: "I make no secret of my Judaism, to which I have not returned, because I never left it." Ask: What do you think Heinrich Heine meant? *(I am openly a Jew and always have been a Jew.)* In what way was Heine's situation similar to the *conversos* of Spain? *(Prejudice made being Jewish a handicap.)* In what way was it different? *(It was not dangerous for Heine to live as a Jew—he voluntarily converted to advance his career.)*

pages 136–137 **Responding to Changing Times: Reform Judaism**

Invite students to read the section in small groups. Based on the text's description of Abraham Geiger's emphasis on prophetic Judaism, challenge each group of students to list as many social justice activities—such as feeding the hungry, attending peace demonstrations, caring for the sick and elderly—as they can. The group that lists the greatest number of activities wins.

You may create a "Social Activism" chart based on the students' responses. List the activities students named down one side and your class roster down the other. Whenever a student reports that he or she has participated in one of the activities, put a check mark next to his or her name. (Additional activities can be added throughout the year.) At the end of the year, a prize or award may be given to the student(s) who have most frequently participated in social action projects.

pages 137–138 **Responding to Changing Times: Conservative Judaism**

Read the text as a class or individually. Divide the class into teams and assign each team a side in a debate on whether or not Hebrew should be eliminated as the language of Jewish prayer. Before the debate begins, give students time to prepare the reasoning behind their points of view. Once each team has presented its views and reasoning, encourage the teams to question one another.

page 139 Map: The Pale of Settlement

Have students work in pairs so that one student can keep the textbook open to the map on page 139 and the other to the map on page 114, as you point out that the territory in which the Jews settled has shifted more to the east, into Russia, and less into Central Europe. Invite students to share the maps with their parents and ask if older family members, such as great-grandparents, had ever lived in these areas.

pages 140–141 New Ideas Arrive

If time permits, screen the movie *Fiddler on the Roof*, or review the story line and have the class listen to several songs from the soundtrack. (You may want to screen the movie as part of a "Family Connection" activity—see page 67 of this teaching guide.) The movie is based on Sholom Aleichem's short story "Tevye the Milkman." It reflects the experience of the small Jewish communities *(shtetls)* in the Pale of Settlement and how the Jews were affected by the changing world around them.

The opening number, "Tradition," clearly defines everyone's role within the family and community and gives a sense of order and stability. The closing song, "Anatevka" (the name of the town), conveys the Jews' need to adjust to harsh circumstances and to the changing times.

You may want to suggest to your director of education that several classes screen the movie. Your students can provide an introduction to the movie based on the material in this section of the text.

page 141 Awake My People

Invite a volunteer to read the poem. Ask: To what does "night" refer? *(difficult times)* To what does "the sun" refer? *(improved living conditions)* What does it mean to have the gates of Eden/Russia open? *(Jews are now permitted to enjoy the goodness that Russia offers.)* What does being called "brother" signify? *(Jews are accepted like all other Russians.)*

page 143 **Then & Now**

Once students have submitted their research you may want to work with them to create an article for your synagogue's newsletter or Web site. The article can be as simple as a series of interesting historical facts, each one headed with the title "Did You Know?" or "It's a Fact!" Or, you can compare older and newer traditions, under the title "Then & Now."

Family Connection

As suggested on page 66 of this teaching guide, you may want to screen *Fiddler on the Roof* for students and their families. Your students can provide an introduction to the movie based on the material in this chapter.

If you hold such an event, take advantage of the community-building opportunity. Begin by welcoming your guests and inviting everyone to introduce him- or herself. You can make the event more festive and encourage people to socialize by serving light refreshments. If you do, check what dietary regulations your synagogue observes and any other food concerns, such as allergies, that may be an issue.

Alternatively, invite students and their families to locate English translations of several of Sholom Aleichem's short stories, using either the Internet or their home, local, or synagogue library. Through your synagogue's hospitality or *bikur ḥolim* committee, connect the families with elderly or housebound congregants who would appreciate a visit and the opportunity to have such stories read to them. Invite students who make such visits to share their experiences with the class.

If students perform such visits, and you have created a "Social Activism" chart similar to the one described in the "Responding to Changing Times: Reform Judaism" section (see page 65 of this teaching guide), then be sure to check off the students' names on the chart.

13 The Rise of Antisemitism

Nationalism and the Search for Scapegoats

textbook pages ***144–153***

Chapter Overview

Despite the legal gains of emancipation and the social gains of assimilation, anti-Jewish prejudice lingered on. This prejudice caused people to question whether Jews were loyal citizens and it undermined pride in Jewish identity. Jews were now confronted by an antisemitism borne of nationalism. In Germany, antisemitism took many forms, including the public use of antisemitic language and the barring of Jews from select hotels and restaurants. In France the Dreyfus Affair became one of the most infamous antisemitic incidents in the late 1800's.

core concepts

- Prejudice cannot be completely erased by legal mandate or by the victim making efforts to assimilate into the larger society.
- The harm antisemitism does includes undermining Jewish identity and pride.

Learning Objectives

Students will be able to

- Explain why some Europeans resented and mistrusted Jews.
- Describe ways in which Jews responded to antisemitism.
- Apply what they have learned to help them address their own prejudices and the prejudices of others.

Teaching Opportunities

Getting Started

Choose two students who are different in some way—for example, a girl and a boy, different color hair, wearing different color shirts or pants—and invite them to the front of the class. (Choose differences that are not likely to touch on personal sensitivities, such as height, weight, or racial background.) Give each student exactly the same type of chair to sit in, the same amount of time (about one minute) to say a few words about him or herself, and the same honorarium of a gold star or some other modest reward for the presentation.

Then say: You might say that I have just treated these two students as equals. They received the same chair, the same amount of time to speak, and the same reward. Does that mean that *they* are exactly the same? (Point out some of the obvious differences.) Help students understand that to treat people with equality does not mean that the people are the same. Rather, to treat people with equality means that you give them access to the same opportunities and rights.

Explain that feelings of prejudice can cause people to fear, disrespect, or mistrust others who are different from them and to deny those people access to the opportunities and rights that are given to others. Tell students that in this chapter, they will learn about the prejudice European Jews experienced in the late nineteenth century and the impact it had on them.

page 145 "Us" and "Them"

Invite two volunteers to read aloud one paragraph each of the text. Then read the following quote aloud: "As long as you keep a person down, some part of you has to be down there, to hold him down, so it means you cannot soar as you otherwise might." Explain that this statement was made by Marian Anderson, an African-American singer who lived from 1897 to 1993, and who had suffered from the indignities of prejudice. Ask: What do you think Anderson meant? *(If you oppress others or try to keep them down in any way, you keep yourself down because you can't become the best person you are capable of being.)*

Ask: How might viewing the world in terms of *them* and *us* be hurtful not only to the people who are defined as outsiders—or "them"—but also to those who are seen as the in group—"us." *(makes the in group fearful of those they see as outsiders; the in group may feel that it needs to live defensively to protect itself; the in group loses the benefits of the abilities and strengths of those they see as outsiders)*

page 146 **Map: Emancipation in Late 19th Century**

Ask: Which country was the first to become emancipated? *(France, 1791)* Which country labeled on this map was the last to emancipate? *(Switzerland, 1874)*

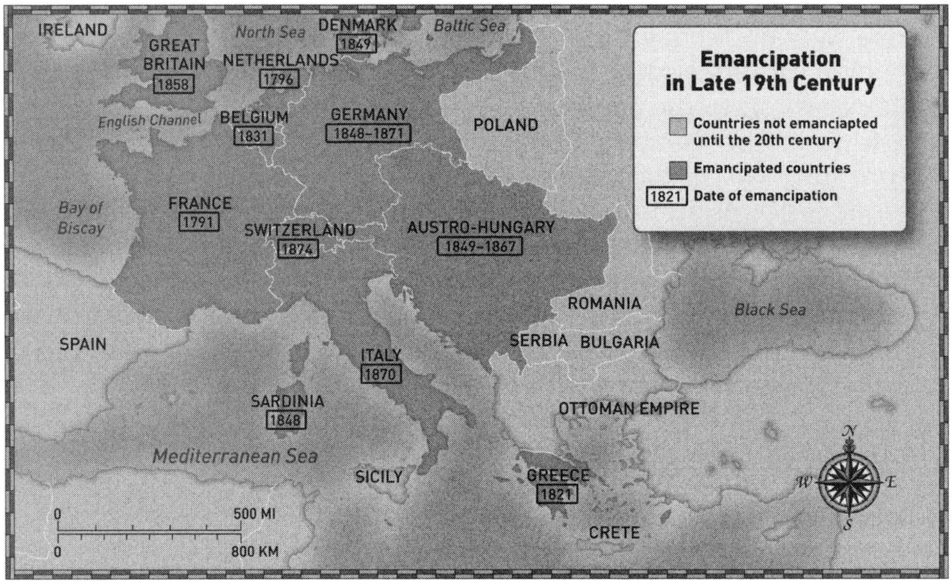

page 147 **Searching for Scapegoats**

Read the section as a class or individually. Ask: If a problem was not caused by the person or group who has been made into a scapegoat, what effect will holding the scapegoat responsible or punishing the scapegoat have on solving the problem? *(It will distract people's attention from the real cause.)* How might accepting that person or group be helpful? *(They might help you figure out a solution; you might become friends.)*

page 149 **Photograph: Girl Receiving Haircut**

Encourage students to share their points of view on when a healthy concern for one's appearance turns into an obsession, or even disrespect for oneself.

pages 149, 151 **The Plague of Self-Doubt**

Invite volunteers to each read aloud one paragraph in the section. As a class, discuss the tendency of those who have experienced prejudice to begin to doubt their self-worth, and sometimes even to develop self-hatred as well as contempt for others in their group. Have students work alone or in partners to create a formula for maintaining one's self-respect in such circumstances. For example:

caring friends + self-confidence + dignity - fear = self-respect

Invite students to share their formulas, then write the following quote from the Book of Psalms on the chalkboard: "I will praise You, God, for I am awesomely and wondrously made. Marvelous are Your works; my soul knows it well" (Psalms 139:14).

Ask: What does the quote mean. *(I'm a terrific person. In my heart, I know I'm a good person—and I look good, too! I thank God for making me as I am.)*

Tell students that those words were written for our ancestors and for every generation after them, including today's and tomorrow's generations. Suggest that to develop a deeper appreciation of themselves, students may want to recite the quote from the Book of Psalms each morning when they wake up or in the middle of the day if they need a quick pick-me-up. Because these words do not apply just to them, tell students that they also can be a reminder to treat others with respect.

page 150 **Famous Figures: Jacques Joseph**

Divide the class into two teams to debate the question of whether Dr. Joseph helped or harmed his patients. Give each team five or ten minutes to prepare their argument. After each team has presented its view, invite students to question one another.

page 152 **You Are There: Cross the Atlantic—Yes or No?**

Possible answers: *Remain in Europe—family and friends, speak the language, surroundings are familiar, can keep your possessions. Set sail for North America—more tolerant society, better financial opportunities for the future, adventure.*

page 153 **Then & Now**

After students have completed the activity and shared their responses, on the chalkboard write the list of student names in alphabetical order. Have students copy the list on a sheet of paper, leaving a few blank lines between each name. (Alternatively, you can create and duplicate the list in advance using a computer.) Next to each name, have students list one or two qualities or skills that they particularly like and respect in that person. For example, a student might write about one student's kindness and good humor, another student's strong ability to read Hebrew and willingness to help others, and a third person's generosity and agility in sports.

Collect the papers and explain to students that this has not only been an opportunity to learn how to focus on other people's strengths but also to learn about the many qualities and skills their classmates appreciate in them. For the next class, collate the information so that you have one sheet for each student that describes his or her strengths. (Do not indicate who the source of each comment was.)

Distribute each sheet to the student it describes. When students receive and read their sheets, you may want to ask if they were surprised by any of the comments and how they felt receiving them or hearing how their own comments had made someone feel.

Family Connection

You may want to suggest that families do a similar activity to the one described in "Then & Now" (page 71 of this teaching guide). Each person can write about the strengths of other family members. Members of the extended family, such as grandparents or cousins, can be included in the activity. Each person can write up to five qualities and skills that they like and respect in the family member. A parent can take responsibility for collating the comments and developing the sheets for each member of the family.

14 U.S. Jewry, 1820–1880

Balancing Freedom and Tradition

textbook pages 154–165

Chapter Overview

The United States provided new opportunities for Judaism and Jewish communities to thrive. As Jews spread out over the United States and experienced the freedom to create an American style of Judaism, the Jewish religion and culture became increasingly diverse. Some Jews chose to completely assimilate into the American culture. Reform Judaism became more innovative, the seeds of Conservative Judaism were sown, and revivalists sought to adapt Judaism to life in America while maintaining traditional Jewish values and customs.

core concepts

- Freedom and economic opportunity created greater diversity in the Jewish community.
- Early Jewish immigrants struggled to balance their modern lives with a commitment to traditional Jewish values.
- Balancing modernization and traditional Jewish values continues to stimulate change and creative adaptation in our own time.

Learning Objectives

Students will be able to

- Describe the differences that arose in beliefs and religious observances within different segments of American Jewry.
- Explain how these differences contributed to the development of American styles of Judaism.
- Apply what they have learned to identify how growing diversity continues to characterize Judaism in North America today.

Teaching Opportunities

Getting Started

Ask: Can you imagine a gunfight between a rabbi and the president of a synagogue over which prayer book to use? Tell students that Rabbi Moses May and Abraham Waldman of Beth Israel in Portland, Oregon, had such a confrontation. The congregation, which was founded in 1859, had a series of religious leaders before Rabbi May had arrived. Services were conducted in the Orthodox tradition, using the prayer book *Minhag Ashkenaz.* (Explain that *minhag* means "custom.") Rabbi May wanted to use *Minhag America,* published by Rabbi Isaac Mayer Wise, but members of the congregation were divided between using *Minhag Ashkenaz* and *Minhag Portland,* which had been created by the synagogue's board of directors.

Waldman, the president-elect of the synagogue, did not want to see the prayer book changed. He and the rabbi had been arguing for years. Finally, their dispute erupted in a fistfight and shoot-out on a Friday morning in October 1880, under the window of the Esmond Hotel, where the president of the United States, Rutherford B. Hayes, was staying.

Rabbi May had been talking to a friend outside the hotel when Waldman came up behind him. Waldman grabbed Rabbi May by the collar and hit him in the face, breaking his glasses. The rabbi pulled out a pistol and shot at his attacker. His first shot missed, but his second shot tore through Waldman's coat. Another man grabbed the rabbi before he could reload and shoot again. (This retelling is based on the account in *The First Rabbi: Origins of Conflict Between Orthodox and Reform: Jewish Polemic Warfare in Pre-Civil War America: A Biographical History* by I. Harold Sharfman [Malibu, Calif.: J. Simon/Pangloss, 1988].)

Ask students: What do the titles of the three prayer books (*Minhag Ashkenaz* [Custom of Ashkenazic Jews], *Minhag America* [Custom of American Jews], and *Minhag Portland* [Custom of Portland Jews]) tell you about the possible differences in views held by the congregants? *(Those who wanted to use* Minhag Ashkenaz *wanted to follow the more traditional customs of Ashkenazic Jews; those who wanted to use* Minhag America *wanted to follow the newer customs of American Jewry; and those who wanted to use* Minhag Portland *wanted to follow the developing customs that were specific to the Portland Jewish community.)*

Tell the class that in this chapter they will learn how differences among the American Jewish communities came about and contributed to the development of today's American style of Judaism, in all its diversity.

pages 155, 157 **Seeking a Fresh Start**

Invite one student to read the text aloud. Ask students to describe some of the changes Abraham Kohn might encounter by moving from Germany to the United States. *(language, style of clothing, people, laws, climate, culture, etiquette)* Write students' responses on the chalkboard. Invite students to discuss how these changes might cause difficulties and why it often takes great courage to leave one country to immigrate to another.

page 156 **You Are There: The High Cost of Earning a Living**

Have a volunteer read this section aloud. Ask: What troubled Abraham Kohn? Do you think that he was lazy?

Remind students that the Talmud teaches that those who do not teach their children to earn a living, teach them to become criminals (see the "What Do You Think?" feature on page 65 of the textbook; also see page 36 of this teaching guide). Explain that the ancient rabbis understood that everyone needs food, clothing, and shelter, and that if as adults we do not have the skills to earn money, we may turn to a life of crime.

You may also want to remind students of Rabbi Eleazar ben Azaryah's teachings, which are discussed on page 46 of this teaching guide (see "Famous Figures: Dolce of Worms"). They highlight the rabbinic underderstanding that people need both to work *and* to perform *mitzvot* in order to live healthy and rewarding lives. Abraham Kohn was concerned that Jews had lost their sense of balance between working and living meaningful lives.

page 156 **You Are There: The High Cost of Earning a Living**

Jewish ritual as comfort: *Feel connected to your roots; would not feel so alone; prayer is grounding; feel part of a Jewish community.* Jewish ritual as burden: *Separates Jews from non-Jews; difficult to find kosher foods and some ritual items, such as a* lulav *and an* etrog *for Sukkot; might lose out on opportunities to make money if observe Shabbat.*

pages 157–158 **Jewish Forty-Niners Hit the Frontier**

After students read and discuss the section in small groups, have them write a perspective journal from the point of view of a Jewish forty-niner. Some subjects you may want to suggest that students write about include their willingness or unwillingness to work on Shabbat, availability of kosher food, language barriers, hearing from the folks back home, how it felt to attend the Rosh Hashanah prayer services in Lewis Franklin's store in 1849. Invite students to read aloud their journal entries.

page 158 **Map: Jewish Communities in the U.S., 1878**

Ask: In 1878, which states had ten or more Jewish communities? *(New York, Pennsylvania, Ohio, Indiana, Louisiana, Illinois, Texas, California)* In what region were most of the smaller communities? *(in the West)* Why? *(Jews started to move west only after the gold rush.)*

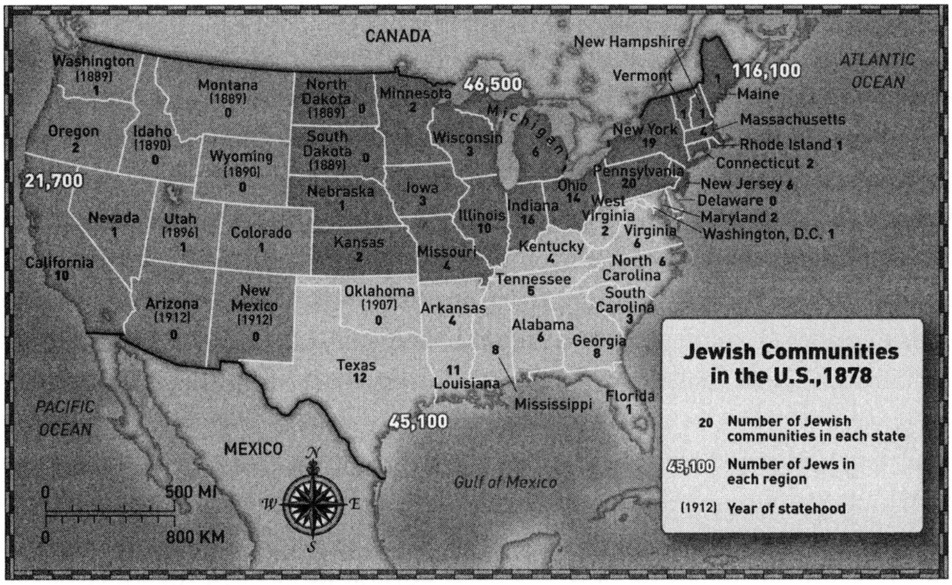

page 159 **Levi's Jeans**

Invite four volunteers to role-play Levi Strauss, Jacob Davis, a Jewish gold miner, and a twenty-first-century descendant of the gold miner. Present the following scenario to students: It is 1873 and the gold miner wants to buy a pair of black cotton pants; Strauss and Davis try to persuade him to buy their blue jeans. The gold miner's descendant exists as a voice in the gold miner's ear, desperately trying to persuade him to buy the jeans. (The descendant wants Strauss to be successful, for if not, jeans might not make it to the twenty-first century.)

page 159 **Photograph: Levi Strauss Advertisement**

After reading and discussing the caption, hand out to each student drawing paper and drawing materials, such as crayons and highlighters. Invite students to design a special edition of a pair of jeans to commemorate the patenting of jeans. Tell them that the patent date of May 20, 1873, was the Jewish date of 23 Iyar 5633.

When students complete their work, create a display, perhaps a bulletin board, for other classes to enjoy. The title might be "Commemorating the Jewish Genes of Jeans."

pages 158–159 **Synagogues Sprout Up**

Both Shearith Israel and B'nei Jeshurun are still strong and active synagogue communities in New York City. Divide your class into two groups and, using the Internet, have each group research one of the two synagogues. Each group can divide the research by assigning members different areas for exploration, such as the history of the synagogue, its current status—including location of the building, names of the rabbi, cantor, and president, number of members—a description of its current religious school, and the types of programs and services it offers including prayer services.

pages 160, 162 **Reform Judaism Evolves**

Have students read this section in small groups or have volunteers read aloud one paragraph each. Remind students that the Rabbi Wise who is mentioned in this section is the same rabbi who published the prayer book that Rabbi May wanted to use (see the "Getting Started" section on page 74 of this teaching guide). Ask: Based on what you have just read, why might some of the more traditional members of Rabbi May's congregation have objected to switching to the *Minhag America* prayer book?

pages 162–163 **From Crisis to Strength**

Invite the director of the local JCC or YM/YWHA to your class to discuss the local history of the organization and to describe the various activities and services it offers. Alternatively, you may want to schedule a tour of one such institution.

page 164 **Famous Figures: Emma Lazarus**

Answer to activity question: *The Reform leaders probably would have strongly disagreed with Lazarus. Many did not identify as members of a separate Jewish people or nation, but only as part of the Jewish religion. This weakened their connection to the Land of Israel.*

page 165 **Photograph: Three Teenagers**

Discuss the photograph and caption with students. If, at the beginning of the book, students wrote about the roles they would like to play in Jewish history (see the "Why Study Jewish History" activity on page 8 of this teaching guide), invite them to revisit what they wrote. Ask them to consider what they might want to change or add to their responses.

If students did not do that activity, invite them to now consider what roles they might want to play in Jewish history and why. Ask them to be specific about the actions they would like to take.

Accommodations for Students with Special Needs

Like most classes, yours probably includes a diverse group of students. Some students may require extra attention to succeed. The activities in this teaching guide are intended for a wide variety of learners and therefore employ a wide variety of modalities. In general, teachers who present material in many different ways will be able to reach many more children.

For children with special learning needs, it is always helpful to find out from parents what accommodations are made for their child in secular school. In addition, consider using one or several of these strategies.

1. Mask parts of the textbook page so that only the activity being taught is visible.

2. Highlight the information in the text to which the students should pay especially close attention.

3. Help students share what they know in ways that are compatible with their learning styles. For example, where appropriate, allow students to answer questions orally instead of writing their answers.

4. Paraphrase and summarize what has been taught. This is helpful for all students.

5. Provide students with special learning needs extra time to finish assignments, or reduce the number of items they are expected to complete.

6. Repeat and define new words and concepts a number of times. Do not assume that students with special needs will recognize them when they see or hear them again later in the class session or the following week.

7. If students have trouble pronouncing new vocabulary, especially terms in Hebrew, model the words and have students repeat them after you.

8. Create a shoe box of flashcards with a key vocabulary word or concept on one side of each card and its definition on the other. Invite children to take the cards home and practice with their parents.

9. Provide opportunities for choral reading rather than asking children to read aloud individually.

10. Set up all students to succeed. When assigning small groups, make sure students with special needs can make a contribution to the group. If they cannot, either choose a different class assignment or provide an alternative learning experience for the students with special learning needs.

11. Reach out to your director of education for suggestions and guidance.

Most importantly, remember that the interpersonal relationships you build and the tone and atmosphere you create in your classroom are as important as the material you teach. Try to be relaxed, respectful and patient with students who have learning challenges. And finally, try to encourage patience and tolerance in all of your students.

NOTES